Jean will never forget the liberation of Paris on 8/25/1944. Every 4th July he takes the opportunity to thank America and the sacrifice of its troops in World War II by taking part in the Ski Valley parade, carrying the old skis and the suitcase he first came with from France.

**To my children: they are, therefore I am!**

# CUISINE ST. BERNARD

## Recipes and reflections from the incomparable mountain inn

**JEAN MAYER & MARIE-PIERRE MOINE**

**Recipes:** Claude Gohard, Christopher Kelly White, Randolph Laird Stabler, Cindie White, Steve White, Patrick Yu, Yann Yven

**Photography:** Peter Lamont

▲

# INTRODUCTION

For years and years it had been the same story: guests asking over and over again for recipes, and Jean running away from committing himself. I used to make a joke of it. Well, with recipes, it's the touch that matters, and it changes all the time–just like the art of loving! Something like that. In fact, I knew that my friends, the guests in our dining room, really wanted to take home with them the essence of what they experienced eating and living with us at the St. Bernard. Then, after many years of skiing together, Claude Roessiger once said to me, why not make a book about the meals at the St. Bernard? You have just the right person staying for a ski week. So I spoke to Marie-Pierre Moine, who was trying to keep up on the slopes with her great friend from school in Paris, Claude's wife Amina. I was in luck, M-P writes cookbooks in London. I saw her *Provence Cooking School* and I liked it very much. I explained that ours could not be just a book about recipes; we needed to incorporate stories, anecdotes about the dining room, the hotel, Taos Ski Valley, with photos that would translate the romance, the entertainment, the fun of eating at the St. B. I wanted the recipes to be people-friendly, fun, and easy to do. The idea is for guests to recreate the meals they enjoyed and share the experience with their friends. I knew that this was risky, that many people interested in a cookbook might feel rather foreign to the emotions I talk about. Yet we feel strongly that good food creates an opportunity for the friendly gathering of mind and spirit, the arts of talking and eating, so we worked on keeping this book very personal to our experiences, with Claude as publisher, only accepting exceptional quality and good taste. Peter Lamont took beautiful photographs, I played *chef d'orchestre*. Our six chefs each contributed their distinct touch and personality. The recipes are from all over the world, with an obvious French touch (can't be helped). Our emphasis at the St. Bernard is on serving the best quality local produce available. I hope you'll do the same thing at home. But what we all really hope is that you have fun cooking, eating and talking about it.

# KACHINA PEAK, THE ST. BERNARD, A LOVE STORY

The St. Bernard's story is a simple one: it begins with the mountain, it lives with the mountain, and it will continue with the mountain. It is the shadow of the peak's long north shoulder that has played with Taos's deep skies and brilliant sun since a time long before the first man came, that held and protected the fine, high-altitude snow that is so odd a visitor to a land of desert horizons, of scrub and tumbleweed and red rock. It is Kachina and its shade that have allowed the ski valley to find this secret corner, the shy *décolleté* that keeps a winter that is foreign to this land so close to its breast, and that reveals it to us, all soft and white and deep, only at the very last moment, after our despair of finding snow at all, as we have wound our way up an often very dry mountain road.

The many tales of the ski valley—of Taos—are a folklore, intertwining myth and reality in what has become a whole fabric of magic, the lovely mountain, the huddle of lodges and funky shops that can only ever be visitors to the valley floor, and the interesting—often remarkable—personages who took the spirit of the mountain upon themselves, a blanket of so many colors, a cover against the storm. Sometimes, around the campfire, we like to hear the retold tales; sometimes, it is time to pass around a new pipe.

Taos was once the mining camp of Twining, with its own funky story, a gang of promoters from New York City who seeded the ground with gold, for a quick buck. There was a hotel—not a bad one—but it soon all came to naught. There was no gold. In 1955, Ernie Blake, Taos's founder, in the sense that he not only forged the ski valley but literally found it, was working at the Santa Fe Ski Basin, but spending his free time in a small plane, with the Indian guide Pete Totemoff. They sought another gold, the perfect mountain, and they discovered it: a unique combination of geography, geology, and exposure. It's the altitude, the terrain, and the north face that made Taos.

The St. Bernard arrived in 1957, eight days before Christmas, when Jean Mayer disembarked from the bus in Taos Village, skis on his shoulder, just

4

...

back to the States from service with the 10th Mountain Division in Germany. He had promoted himself to the head of the ski patrol in Garmisch, after a distinctly unsuitable first posting in the flatlands that surround Frankfurt. And, already then, the people who would have a role in making Taos were in some way in touch, even if only by the touching of their spirits, their dreams, and their wills. This isn't a history, and we will only ask forgiveness from those who aren't named, but let us remember those who are: Bill Judd, Al Rosen, Chilton Anderson, Giuseppe Olmi, Georgia Hotton, Christian Pravda, Pete Seibert, Sepp Ruschp, Mickey Blake, Gordon Briner ... names known and names less known, all with stories that are a part of this story. And, there is Jean's family.

Monsieur and Madame Mayer, Jean's parents, came to Taos from France with their son Dadou, in 1960. Jean, a graduate of l'Ecole Hôtelière had nicked the job of technical director of the ski school from an avowedly better skier, but in a newly established resort—more the hope of a resort, at the time— the greatest asset was to have more than one skill! The Hotel St. Bernard was born the same year, its early success guaranteed by Jean, its French proprietor, who very naturally set up co-ed dorms, not thinking to shock— and titillate—American innocence! Taos was made by a small group of strong-willed, self-reliant individuals, as are now too few, men and women who brought all of themselves to the valley. In Jean there was, to be sure, a remarkable skier, an athlete who understands the relationship not only between ski and snow, but between man and mountain, in a way given to few. But, also, a disciplined hotelier, a joyful chef, a reader of philosophy, a cowboy—well, okay, a French cowboy—an inspiration to the young, a musician, a cool dude, a loyal patron, a friend, and a great father: Michael, professor of international economics; Sacha, renowned personal trainer and musician; Ryan, physical therapist UNM; Monique, Secretary of Tourism for New Mexico; Kihei, finishing his master's in architecture; Krizia,

...

graduate of William Smith College in international relations, lately at her father's side at the St. Bernard; Kailani, back from a year in Paris, resuming her art studies at UNM; Kody (pictured with Krizia on previous page), at the Taos Academy. Special, non?

And, who can tell this story without the food? There was always Jean, as there is to this day. At first, with the help of a woman from the Pueblo, he was chef. Then came Yvon Silvé, followed by the inimitable Claude Gohard, *qui a fait la marque*, literally, who "made the brand" of "La Cuisine St. Bernard". The story cannot be complete without recognizing all who followed, accomplished, refined—however funky—and dedicated. What would the food be without the presentation, always so personal, by Jean himself, at each table, accompanied by a story and a description that some, apparently, even believe ... ?

A great hotel is made by a spirit, given to it by the one who has made it, and maintained by a great staff: fifty-five dedicated members, some into a second generation, with an average of seventeen years of individual service. This alone says more than extra words might. Guests are into a fourth generation. Finally, there is the spirit. It is a flame, durable and strong in the mountain, always fragile in human hands, so dependent upon the human soul. That is the story of Taos: a fascinating, great, silent mountain—did you never walk away from the lights in the winter night to listen to the mountain?—and the men who came to this high and narrow Sangre de Cristo valley, from so many lives, from around the world. It's about the mountain.

*Claude Roessiger*

# SATURDAY

**BIENVENUE LES AMIS**

"I want people to feel they are at home from the moment they arrive. What matters is to make them comfortable as quickly as possible. There's always a bit of chaos with people coming and going, but we want our guests to feel welcome and at ease. Now you know you are in the right place... I often say that when I bring the soup to the tables at dinner. Saturday night at the St. B is not the time for experimenting with new dishes: I choose a menu many people will be familiar with. I do it on purpose. The dishes should be like old friends guests have been long-ing to see again. We always try to make the menu better than ever be-fore. It's important for guests to experience right away the quality of what they'll enjoy throughout their stay. If they go to sleep with a happy feeling on the first evening, the week is off to a good start. For Cuisine St. Bernard, we have selected recipes from a menu for a ski week breakfast, lunch and dinner, with wine suggestions following the dinner menu. You will find a full index at the end of the book."

# ON THE DECK

If the sun is shining, and—it being in Taos Ski Valley New Mexico—the odds are in favor of this happening, the deck at the St. B will be buzzing on any Saturday of the season. Saturday is change-over day, there is no lunch in the dining room, the atmosphere in the hotel around the middle of the day can only be described as very mildly chaotic, so the deck is the best place to stay while, somehow, order is gently being restored below. Incoming guests rush up the steps to breathe in the air and look up at the glorious view of the mountains in happy anticipation; old acquaintances just recognize each other; friendships are renewed; weekend skiers relax over a hamburger or a Taos Frito Pie and a beer; departing visitors. who have finished ski-week but can't quite bear to leave, linger on quietly for a soup after those last few extra runs. The deck menu is simple, comfortable, well executed, and catering for hungry people who want their food served quickly and without fuss. Regulars will tell you that the Chili Con Carne is part of the tradition and second to none, while for many the Tortilla Soup is the only way to start another week at the St. B.

# TORTILLA SOUP

*Serves 8-10.*
*Preparation and cooking*
*40 minutes.*

· **2 tablespoons olive oil**
· **1 large white onion, minced**
· **1 cup mild green chiles, chopped**
· **2 cloves garlic, crushed**
· **1 large can crushed tomatoes**
· **1 can beef broth**
· **1 can chicken broth**
· **1 large can tomato juice**
· **pinch cumin**
· **pinch red chile powder**
· **¼ cup lime juice**
· **¼ cup tequila**
· **3-4 tablespoons chopped cilantro**
· **2 cups cooked chicken meat, diced**
· **salt and pepper**

**To serve:**
· **tortilla chips, crushed**
· **2 cups (225g) grated**
**Cheddar cheese**

**Fragrant, warming, and an irresistible party dish, this soup is really easy to put together.**

**1** Put a large pot over a medium heat, add the olive oil, sauté the onion, green chile, and garlic, stirring, for 3-5 minutes until softened.

**2** Add the crushed tomatoes, beef broth, chicken broth, and tomato juice. Stir, add the cumin and red chile powder. Simmer for 10 minutes.

**3** Add the lime juice, tequila, and cilantro, and bring back to a simmer.

**4** Add the chicken and return to a simmer. Adjust the seasoning.

**5** Serve very hot over crushed tortilla chips and cheese.

**St. B tip:** If you need to smash several garlic cloves, wrap them in plastic wrap and flatten with the flat of a cleaver or large knife.

# CLAUDE'S CHILI CON CARNE

*Serves 6.*
*Preparation and cooking 1 hour.*

· 2 tablespoons olive oil, plus
extra for greasing
· 1 pound (450g) ground
hamburger beef, broken up
· ½ white onion, diced
· 6 garlic cloves, crushed
· 2 tablespoons tomato paste
· 1 tablespoon Chimayo chile powder
· 1 tablespoon ground
coriander seeds
· 1 tablespoon brown sugar
· 1 tablespoon chopped basil
· 1 tablespoon ground oregano
· 1 bay leaf, crushed
· ½ tablespoon ground cumin
· ½ tablespoon paprika
· 4 tablespoons canned
crushed tomato
· 1 ounce (30g) Jalapeños, diced
(fresh, canned, frozen and defrosted)
· ½ cup Dos Equis or other Mexican beer
· 1 cup beef stock, plus extra as needed
· 1 cup Mexican canned chile beans
· 1 cup canned kidney beans
· 1 cup pinto beans
· salt and pepper

French chefs, beware of hot spices... When Claude Gohard first came to New Mexico, he rejected chiles as a matter of principle: "Much too fiery for good cooking. I vowed I'd never use them. But somehow they're quite addictive and now I love cooking with chile". Over the years, Claude's take on the classic dish has addicted thousands of skiers and the St. B's Chili Con Carne is a hot favorite on the deck. His recipe is meaty and, unlike many versions, ungreasy; he also uses liquid from the canned beans to bind the stew. Salt only gets added at the last minute if needed. And a sip or two of the beer is the cook's perk.

1 Lightly oil a large frying pan, then put over a high heat. Spread the beef in the pan, and sauté over a high heat for at least 8 minutes, stirring and smashing down with the back of a large spoon. Fry until the fat runs out, tip the beef into a colander, strain well, and reserve.

2 Add the olive oil to the pan, tip in the onion, and sauté for 3-5 minutes until softened. Tip in the beef and reduce the heat. Add the garlic, tomato paste, and chile powder, and sauté for 15 minutes, stirring frequently.

3 Sprinkle in the coriander, sugar, basil, oregano, bay leaf, cumin, and paprika. Stir and sauté for 15 minutes.

4 Add the crushed tomato, jalapeño, beer, and stock. Stir well, add the beans and half the liquid from the cans. Bring to a boil, reduce the heat a little, and simmer for 10–15 minutes, adding a little more stock if the mixture looks too dry. Adjust the seasoning before serving.

**St. B tips:** Add chile and hot spices a little at a time. You can always add more but you can't take them out. Taste as you cook, and adjust seasonings to suit your palate. You can chill, or better still freeze, leftover chili—it's worth making double quantities. Always bring back to a boil before eating, and add stock if it looks dry. Never add water—it will dilute the taste.

# FRENCH ONION SOUP

*Serves 6-8.*
*Preparation and cooking*
*1½-2 hours.*

· *2* sticks (250g) butter
· *10* red onions, sliced
· *10* yellow onions, sliced
· *2* tablespoons balsamic vinegar
· *2* cups (480ml) red wine
· *2* quarts (2l) white vegetable stock (see opposite)
· *1* sachet bouquet garni
· *1* sprig fresh rosemary
· *2* cloves garlic, crushed
· *½* cup cognac
· sea salt and *12* freshly crushed white peppercorns


**To serve:**
· *6* thick slices farm bread or baguette
· *6* tablespoons grated Swiss or French Gruyère

**Classic recipes for the great** *gratinée à l'oignon* **use chicken stock, but Yann likes to make a vegetarian version that tastes just as good if not better. Veggies and meat-eaters alike, everyone can enjoy it. It's also a good reason to prepare White vegetable stock–it takes a bit of time, but it's worth it. And both the stock and the soup can be prepared ahead.**

**1** In a wide heavy pan over medium heat, melt the butter. Add the onions and cook until golden brown, stirring occasionally with a wooden spoon. Turn up heat to high, add 2 tablespoons water, stir well, and add the balsamic vinegar. Stir and scrape for 2 minutes. Reduce heat to low and cook for 10 minutes. Return heat to high, add red wine, stir, and scrape until thick and syrupy.

**2** Reduce the heat to a minimum, stir in the stock, sachet bouquet garni, rosemary, and garlic. Still stirring, turn up heat and bring to a boil, cover partly, reduce heat, and simmer gently for 45 minutes, stirring from time to time. Take off heat, cover, and let stand until ready to finish.

**3** Approximately 30 minutes before serving, stir in the cognac and season with sea salt and white pepper. Turn up heat to medium, and bring soup to a light simmer for 10–15 minutes, until the alcohol has evaporated.

**4** Meanwhile, lightly toast the bread. Spread the Gruyère on top, and broil until bubbly. Float on top of the soup. Serve hot.

**Serve St. B style :** Bring the steaming soup to the table in a big tureen or pot and dish out with a ladle.

# WHITE VEGETABLE STOCK

*Makes 3 quarts (3l).*
*Preparation and cooking*
*1¼ hours.*

· *3 tablespoons olive oil*
· *10 shallots, slivered*
· *4 garlic cloves, slivered*
· *3 tablespoons chopped parsley*
· *3-4 sprigs thyme*
· *2-3 sprigs oregano*
· *3 teaspoons dried chervil*
· *6 parsnips, roughly chopped*
· *6 celery stalks, roughly chopped*
· *2 tablespoons dry sherry*
· *12 white peppercorns*

**Don't be put off by the time this lovely stock takes to make: it's not difficult, it's light, and it smells and tastes subtly wonderful. Worth making extra: leftovers can be chilled or frozen, ready to turn sauces, stews, and soups into class acts.**

**1** In a large pot, heat the olive oil over medium heat, tip in the shallot and garlic, and cook for 10 minutes until tender and golden, stirring frequently. Add the fresh herbs and chervil. Stir in 2 tablespoons water, add the parsnips and celery, and cook for 5 minutes.

**2** Turn up heat to high. Add sherry and peppercorns, and deglaze. Stir and scrape until absorbed. Reduce heat to very low, cook for 15 minutes.

**3** Add 3 quarts (3l) water, turn up heat, bring to a boil, reduce heat a little, and simmer for 30 minutes. Take off heat, cover, and let it stand for 10 minutes, Strain through a fine sieve.

# RIB-EYE STEAK

*with sauce au poivre*

*Serves 6-8.*
*Preparation, resting steak, and cooking 1 hour.*

· *2–3 pounds (900g–1.5 kilos) rib eye steak*
· *3 cloves garlic, smashed with flat of a knife*
· *2 sticks (250g) butter*
· *1 tbsp dried Mediterranean herbs or herbes de Provence*
· *pinch of salt for each side of steak*
· *pinch of pepper for each side of steak*

**Top-quality steak is expensive and you want to get the cooking just right. The St. B chefs have had years of practice determining when steak is done to perfection. They use the touching technique.... When you poke it with a finger, rare steak should feel like the fleshy part near the base of your thumb, nice and relaxed. For medium-rare that fleshy part feels like it does when your thumb and pointer finger lightly touch together. Medium-well feels like it does when you are pushing thumb and pointer finger together. And you might prefer the juice reading method... When the steak is rare, there are no juices in the pan except the butter. Blood surfaces when the meat is medium-rare (because it is being pushed out of the steak), and coagulated blood (grayish matter) and some clear liquid both appear when the steak is well-done, due to all moisture leaving the meat. Lesson over... enjoy your perfectly cooked steak.**

**1** Melt the butter in small saucepan, add the garlic and herbs, and simmer for 5 minutes over a low heat. Leave to cool to room temperature.

**2** One hour before serving, brush the steaks with the seasoned butter. Season each side with salt and pepper.

**3** Heat a large cast-iron pan just to smoking point. Lay the steak in the pan, and cook each side on a high heat 2-5 minutes, depending on thickness and desired degree of cooking (see above). Leave to settle for a few minutes before slicing.

**St B tip:** Be sure not to crowd steaks in your pan or cooking surface. This produces steaming, which makes it tough for browning to occur. Instead, cook in batches. It's also a good idea to pull the steak out of the pan to allow the pan to recover some heat, and wait until it starts smoking again before you put the steak back in the pan.

# SAUCE AU POIVRE

*Serves 6-8.*
*Preparation and cooking*
*30 minutes.*

· *1* small can green peppercorns with *1* tablespoon of their liquid
· *½* cup (120ml) dry white wine
· *1* cup (240ml) stock (beef, vegetable, chicken, mushroom)
· splash of cognac
· pinch of thyme
· *2* mushrooms, thinly sliced then chopped
· *1* tablespoon (50g) butter
· *1* small shallot, minced (if you like)
· pinch red pepper
· *1* cup (240ml) heavy cream
· salt and pepper

This is a Jean favorite and an all-time great, best with a French entrecote cooked medium-rare, preferably with a glass of fruity Saint Joseph. He likes to use green peppercorns from Madagascar: "They are the best. When I say that to people they laugh at me, but when they taste the sauce, they understand." If you can't find the real thing, a small can of green peppercorns will do very well. And you can use the stock from "whatever you are cooking".

1  Simmer the peppercorns and juice with the white wine, stock, cognac and a pinch of thyme.

2  In a frying pan, over medium heat, cook the mushrooms with the butter, shallot (if you like), red pepper until soft. Add the cream, and heat gently.

3  Blend everything together. Adjust the seasoning. Serve hot with the steak.

# AVOCADO SALAD

*with sweet red onions & lime*

*Serves 6-8.*
*Preparation and marinating*
*1 hour.*

**The sweet red onion and the zingy dressing can be used to accompany other dishes. Chris has 'deconstructed' his salad recipe to make it easier to prepare the ingredients separately.**

**For the sweet red onion garnish:**
· **½ red onion, very thinly sliced (on a mandolin if you have one)**
· **rice wine vinegar to cover**

**For the sweet red onion garnish:**

**1** Cover the sliced onions with rice vinegar. Leave for 1 hour before using. If you like, cover and refrigerate for up to 3 weeks.

**For the avocado salad:**
· *2-3* **ripe avocadoes, halved**
· **pinch of salt**
· **juice of** *1* **lime**

**For the avocado salad:**

**2** Slice each halved avocado into four. Remove the skin and put the flesh in a bowl, sprinkle over the salt and lime juice. Toss gently and cover.

**For the dressing:**
· *1* **teaspoon sesame oil**
· **⅔ cup (160ml) extra virgin first cold press olive oil**
· **⅓ cup (80ml) apple cider vinegar**
· **pinch of red chile, preferably chimayo**
· *1-2* **teaspoon(s) soy sauce**
· **juice and finely grated zest** *1* **unwaxed lemon**
· *1* **garlic clove, minced**
· **leaves from a few sprigs of fresh mint or basil, or rosemary**

**For the dressing:**

**3** Combine all ingredients, and blend. Store leftover dressing in a jar in the refrigerator for up to 3 weeks. Shake before use.

**To finish the salad:**

**4** Put 3 tablespoons dressing in a shallow bowl. Add the arugula, and toss gently. Add the avocado and the onion, and finish off with a little more dressing (if needed) and a crank of black pepper.

**St. B tip**: Always go easy with salad dressing. You don't want to drench the leaves and you can always add a little extra later.

**To finish the salad:**
· *3-4* **handfuls baby arugula leaves, washed and drained**
· **black pepper**

# MOUNTAIN BERRY TART

*Serves 6.*
*Preparation 20 minutes.*

· **1 blind baked tart pastry shell**
· **2½ cups (600ml) pastry cream**
**(see recipe opposite)**
· **mixed berries:**
**1 cup blueberries, ½ cup each**
**raspberries and blackberries**
· **handful strawberries, hulled and**
**halved if large**

**1** Spread the pastry cream evenly over the base of the tart shell. Arrange the berries on top, ending up with the strawberries. If you like, fan out the strawberries before putting on the tart. Plant a few toothpicks into the tart, cover with cling film, and refrigerate until ready to serve.

**2** Serve with a little Chantilly (see below).

# CHANTILLY

*Serves 6.*
*Preparation 10 minutes.*

· **2 cups (480ml) chilled good-**
**quality heavy cream**
· **2-3 tablespoons light brown sugar**
· **1 vanilla pod, split in half (or ½**
**teaspoon Madagascar vanilla extract)**

**1** Put the cream and sugar in a mixing bowl. Whisk until fluffed up with soft peaks.

**2** Using the tip of a small narrow knife or a pointed teaspoon, scrape the black seeds and pulp from the vanilla pod. Stir this or the vanilla extract into the cream.

# PASTRY CREAM

*Makes 1 qt (1l).*
*Preparation and cooking 1 hour.*

· **¾ cup (100g) cornstarch**
· *1* **quart (1l) whole milk**
· *1* **cup (225g) granulated sugar**
· *2* **whole large free-range eggs**
**and** *8* **yolks**
· *1* **stick (115g) unsalted butter**
· *1* **tablespoon Madagascar vanilla**
**extract or seeds and pulp from**
**fresh pods**


**WINE SUGGESTIONS:**
A fruity Saint Joseph with the steak,
or a Woodbridge Cabernet Merlot.

**Yann's classic crème pâtissière ('crème pat' for short) is rich, velvety, and not difficult to make. The secret is not to rush it–slowly does it.**

**1** Put the cornstarch into a bowl, add ½ cup (120ml) milk. Stir until all is absorbed and smooth. Put the rest of the milk in a medium large saucepan with the sugar, bring to a gentle boil over medium heat, stirring well with a wooden spoon. Take off the heat.

**2** In a second bowl, whisk together the whole eggs and yolks. Very slowly add the cornstarch mixture, stirring constantly. Pour about two-thirds of the just-boiled milk into the eggs, whisk in well.

**3** Return the egg and milk to the saucepan, cook over medium heat, mixing all the time with a whisk. Carry on cooking and whisking for 10-12 minutes, until thickened. The cooked pastry cream should no longer look like a liquid.

**4** Take off the heat, pour through a fine mesh sieve into a rinsed-out clean bowl.

**5** In a separate bowl, put the diced butter and mix in the vanilla. Pour in the sieved cream. Stir constantly for 2 minutes. Leave to cool to room temperature for about 20 minutes. Place plastic wrap over the cream (not over the bowl to avoid air gaps). Refrigerate for at least 3 hours before serving.

**St. B tip:** Yann recommends using a clean finger to stir the cornstarch into the milk – this way you'll notice any small lumps.

# SUNDAY

**THE SKI-OFF**

"Sunday morning is ski-off time, and a very important moment in the ski week. Many people feel a bit nervous about being watched and judged by so many pairs of eyes when they haven't got their ski legs back. One thing we do is to nurture our guests with a proper eggs benedict breakfast. This never fails to help them get them off to a good start. The ski-off itself we try to make as friendly as possible. Really, it is very guest-centered. What matters to us instructors is for the placement to reflect people's wishes, not just their ability on the slopes. We want them to feel at ease, and to enjoy what ski school has to offer and the company of their fellow skiers. Guests come back to a balanced lunch that's very European in style–carefully planned and prepared but nothing complicated: a soup and a quiche, followed by fresh fruit. Dinner is colorful and aromatic. Borscht and a shot of vodka make everyone relax. Since there was steak last night, we serve wild salmon with aïoli, the aromatic garlic mayo of Provence. And dessert is a large lavender-flavored chocolate truffle. When it comes to sweet endings and chocolate I believe in quality rather than quantity!"

# EGGS BENEDICT

*Serves 6.*
*Preparation and cooking*
*35 minutes.*

· *6 slices Canadian bacon*
· *3 English muffins, split in halves*
· *6 very fresh free-range eggs*
· *2 quarts (2l) water*
· *½ cup (120ml) white vinegar*
· *1 medium tomato, diced or finely chopped*
· *¼ cup (4 tablespoons) freshly chopped flat-leaf parsley*

**For the lemon and lime hollandaise:**
· *2 yolks from very fresh free-range eggs*
· *1 cup (225g) clarified butter (see St. B. tip page 42)*
· *2 tablespoons fresh lemon juice*
· *2 tablespoons fresh lime juice*
· *1 teaspoon sea salt*
· *½ teaspoon ground black pepper*

**Whoever Mr Benedict was – the origin of the culinary classic is still fiercely debated – he may rest happily in his grave. His fabulous dish is safe at the St. B. The inn's delicious take on the old favorite has everyone lining up for breakfast bright and early on ski-off Sunday morning.**

**1** First make the hollandaise sauce: put the egg yolks in small bowl that fits over a small saucepan. Whisk the yolks until smooth and dull in appearance. Put water in the pan and heat until simmering, then place the egg yolk bowl over the pan, making sure it does not touch the water. Whisk the eggs over the simmering water for 2-3 minutes. Remove the pan from the heat and continue whisking.

**2** Put the butter in a small pan and carefully heat until it's the same temperature as a hot shower. Very slowly drizzle the warm liquid butter into the yolks, while continuously whisking. Increase the drizzle to a trickle, continue whisking in the butter until you have used half. Trickle in the lemon and lime juice, and the rest of the butter, a little at a time, at the same speed until finished, still whisking.

**3** Remove the bowl from pan, season mixture with salt and pepper. Cover and keep warm while you cook the bacon and poach the eggs. Sauté the bacon in a pan over medium-high heat until each side is seared and light brown. Remove from the heat and keep warm. Toast the English muffins and butter them.

**4** To serve, place the bacon over the buttered split muffins, top with poached eggs, and cover with the hollandaise. Garnish with the tomato and parsley, and serve as soon as possible.

# STEVE'S 3 CHEESE QUICHE

*Serves 10-12.*
*Cooking and preparation*
*1½ hours.*

· *5 medium free-range eggs*
· *1½ cups (350ml) heavy cream*
· *½ teaspoon sea salt*
· *¼ teaspoon ground pepper*
· *2 tablespoons olive oil*
· *½ medium onion, finely diced*
· *2-3 cloves garlic*
· *½ cup (120ml) dry white wine*
· *¼ lb (125g) sliced bacon*
· *¼ lb (125g) baby spinach leaves*
· *½ cup (50g) each grated*
**Alpenzeller, Gruyère and Emmental**
**cheese**
· *2 deep dish 9 in (22.5cm) part-*
**baked pie shells**

**Try serving this convivial quiche at a buffet brunch with one of the St.B salad recipes, such as Patrick's Belgian Endive and Tomato Salad (page 104).**

**1** Preheat the oven to 375ºF (190ºC, gas mark 5). Beat the eggs in a mixing bowl until smooth. Add the cream with some salt and pepper. Whisk vigorously until well blended.

**2** In a sauté pan, heat the oil over medium-high heat, toss in the onion and garlic. Sauté for 2-3 minutes. Add the wine, stir and cook for a further 2-3 minutes. Remove from the heat and set aside.

**3** Sauté the bacon in a pan over medium-high heat until each side is seared and light brown. Cool and cut to bite-size pieces.

**4** Add the onion mixture, bacon, spinach, and grated cheeses to the mixing bowl. Mix well. Adjust the seasoning.

**5** Pour into the pie shells and bake for 45 minutes–1 hour, until the centers of the quiches no longer wobble when you shake them. Let rest at least ½ hour on a cooling rack before serving.

**St. B tip:** Remember cheese is salty and do not over-salt the filling.

# FRESH FRUIT AND HONEY

*Serves 6-8.*
*Preparation 15 minutes.*

· **1½ pounds (700g) seasonal fruit of your choice**
· **¼ cup (125ml) port or sweet vermouth**
· **1 cup (240ml) plain yogurt**
· **¼ cup (60ml) honey or agave**

**Few people can resist prepared fresh fruit. The peeling and coring work is done for them and it's the simplest, healthiest, and lightest of desserts. Berries, melons, apples, oranges, clementines, kiwi, banana, star fruit, ripe mango, a dash of lime or lemon juice... the choice is yours and the combinations are endless.**

**1** Peel and core the fruit where required, cut into attractive bite-size pieces. Place in a shallow bowl, drizzle over the port or vermouth and gently stir together. Let stand about 30 minutes.

**2** Just before serving, mix together the yogurt and honey or agave, drizzle over the fruit, and serve immediately.

▲

# JEAN AND STEVE SPOT A PROBLEM

Some people will tell you that it takes four hundred years of rolling and mowing for an English lawn to be perfect. The process has been somewhat faster for the St. Bernard which has grown and been nurtured into a smooth maturity in its five decades. But high altitude, snow and abrupt changes in temperature aren't exactly kind to buildings, and maintenance has to be ongoing. It is an onerous process and a constant source of preoccupation for Jean. He favors small changes rather than drastic measures – much more in keeping with the spirit of the place, but he adds ruefully that sometimes it's much more expensive to improve and maintain than to pull down and start again. During the season there's only time for meticulous cleaning and urgent repairs. Copper pots and surfaces get a proper scrubbing once a week until they gleam, wood is thoroughly polished. The heavy duty serious repairs take place in summer when many-talented Taoseños put their range of different skills to good use-painting furniture, stencilling chests of drawers, shoring up steps... As Jean says, with the passing of years, charm and beauty tend to become become very high maintenance.

# RUSSIAN BORSCHT

*with vodka*

*Serves 4-6.*
*Preparation and cooking*
*3½ hours.*

· *2 short ribs or beef shank*
**(recommended but optional)**
· *10 cups vegetable stock (see*
**Yann's recipe page 19) or stock**
**made from good concentrate**
· *4 tablespoons butter*
· *3 cups (675g) diced beets*
· *1 Vidalia onion, diced*
· *1 large carrot, peeled and diced*
· *2 celery stalks, sliced*
· *2 tablespoons tomato paste*
· *2 tablespoons brown sugar*
· *¼ cup (60ml) red wine vinegar*
· **salt and pepper**
· *¼ cup (700g) chopped parsley*
· *¼ teaspoon dried dill*
· *1 teaspoon dried thyme*
· *1 teaspoon ground*
**cardamom (optional)**
· *1 cup (100g) shredded Napa or*
**Chinese cabbage**
· *2 tablespoons finely chopped parsley*

**For the crème fraîche garni:**
· *¼ cup (60ml) heavy cream*
· *¾ cup (180ml) sour cream*
· **splash of vodka**

**This truly magnificent soup Jean carries in with a big grin and shot glasses of chilled vodka. Don't let the long cooking time put you off trying this recipe: most of it is simmering, there's less than 30 minutes of actual kitchen work involved... perfect bad weather cooking.**

**1** Put the ribs or shank and the stock in a 6-8 quart (6-8l) stock pot. Bring to a boil and simmer gently for 2 hours over low heat.

**2** Strain and reserve the stock. Add the butter to the pot and melt over medium high heat. Add the beets and sauté until the juices run out. Add the onion, stir, and cook 2 minutes. Add the carrots, celery, tomato paste, and sugar. Stir and cook for 4 minutes. Add the vinegar, seasoning, parsley, dill, thyme, and cardamom, if using. Stir.

**3** Add the reserved stock, cover, bring to simmer, reduce heat and simmer gently for 45 minutes-1 hour, until the beets are tender. Taste and adjust the seasoning. You can prepare the soup ahead to this stage and reheat before finishing.

**4** While the soup is simmering, prepare the crème fraîche garni. In a bowl, mix the heavy cream and sour cream, and stir in a good splash of vodka.

**5** Add the cabbage to the hot soup, stir and cook for 5 minutes. Taste and adjust the seasoning. Serve in warmed bowls with a generous dollop of crème fraîche garni and a sprinkling of parsley.

# PAN-FRIED WILD SALMON

*with aïoli sauce*

*Serves 6.*
*Preparation and cooking*
*40 minutes.*

· juice of ½ medium lemon
· juice of ½ medium lime
· *1 tablespoon white wine*
· ½ teaspoon sea salt
· ¼ teaspoon white pepper
· *6 X 6oz* (175g) skinned wild
salmon fillets
· ⅔ cup (150g) clarified butter
(see St. B tip)
· *2 tablespoons chopped fresh dill*
or *1 tablespoon dried dill*

For serving:
· aïoli sauce (see opposite)

**Randy's recipe works every time – it is as foolproof as it is delicious. The secret to cooking the salmon evenly is to allow the center of the fillets time to come to room temperature before you start– it will take a little longer than for the outside.**

**1** In a cup, combine the lemon and lime juice, white wine, salt and pepper. Lightly rub the mixture all over the salmon portions. Cover and leave at room temperature for at least 30 minutes or until the salmon is at room temperature.

**2** Heat a large frying pan over medium-high heat, add the clarified butter. Once the butter is just bubbling, place the salmon in the pan. Cook 2-3 minutes, until the salmon surface is golden brown. Turn over with a fish slice and cook for 2 minutes more.

**3** Lift the salmon onto warmed plates with a fish slice or slotted spoon. Put a healthy dollop of aïoli sauce on top of each fillet, garnish with a large pinch of fresh dill or a slightly smaller pinch of dried.

**St.B tip:** To make clarified butter, melt 4 sticks unsalted butter in a heavy saucepan over low heat. Take off heat, cool a few minutes, use a spoon to skim off the fatty surface foam. Carefully pour the clear liquid butter into a cup, stopping before you get to the sediments at the bottom of the pan. Leave to get cold, cover and refrigerate for up to 3 weeks.

# AIOLI SAUCE

*Makes 2 cups.*
*Bringing to room temperature*
*and preparation 40 minutes.*

· **2–3 cloves garlic, crushed**
· **juice ½ lemon**
· **1 teaspoon white wine**
· **½ teaspoon salt**
· **¼ teaspoon pepper**
· **yolks of 2 very fresh medium free-range eggs**
· **2 cups (480ml) olive oil or 1 cup (240ml) each light-flavored oil and olive oil**

**This garlic-scented mayo is a great partner for fish, cold chicken, boiled potatoes, and hard-cooked eggs.**

**1** Combine the garlic, lemon juice, white wine, salt, and pepper in a bowl.

**2** Cover the egg yolks and leave 15-30 minutes to come to room temperature.

**3** Add the yolks to the bowl. Place a mat of dampened kitchen paper to hold the bowl in place. Whisk vigorously until smooth and no longer shiny. Drizzle in the oil very slowly while still whisking. Once you have whisked in about half the oil, and the sauce has thickened and emulsified, gradually increase the drizzling to a trickle, still whisking. The texture should be like mayo.

**4** Cover and refrigerate. Serve with the Pan-fried wild salmon.

**St. B tip:** If you notice the mixture getting very shiny or beginning to separate, do not panic. Put 1½ teaspoons very cold water in a second bowl. Very slowly drip the aïoli mixture into the water, while whisking fast and furiously. Once the mixture starts binding, increase the dripping rate a little. As soon as it looks set again, slowly whisk in the rest of the mixture.

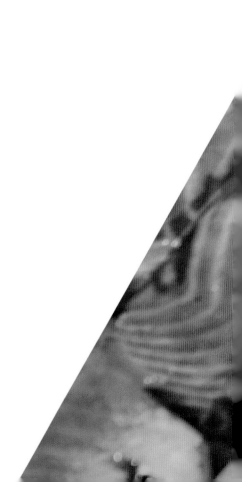

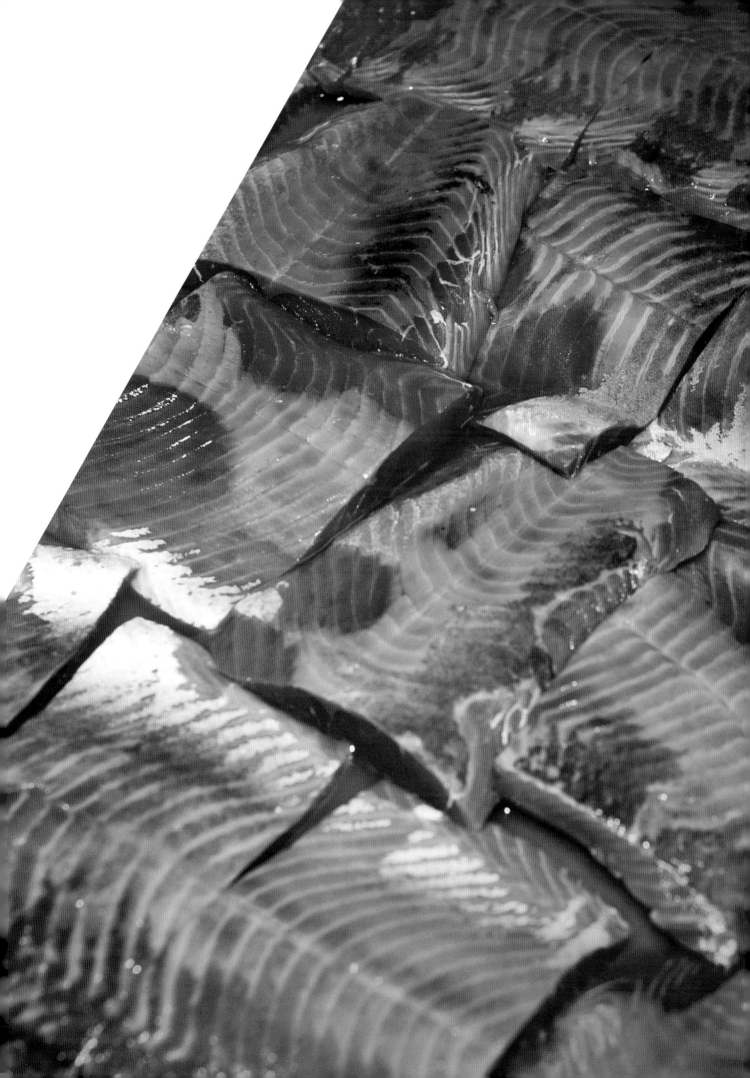

# PERUVIAN QUINOA

*with snow peas and carrot julienne*

*Serves 4-6.*
*Preparation and cooking*
*20 minutes.*

· **4 cups (1l) light stock or water**
· **2 cups (100g) quinoa, rinsed**
· **2 teaspoons salt**
· **snow peas and carrot julienne**
**(see below)**

**High in protein, gluten-free, and a good source of fiber, magnesium and iron, quinoa was a staple of the pre-Columbian Andean diet long before it became the darling of trendy nutritionists. The St. B's colorful garnish of sautéed snow peas and carrot matchsticks turns it into a class act and a lovely side dish.**

**1** In a saucepan, bring the stock or water to a boil over high heat. Add the quinoa and salt, reduce the heat, cover, and simmer for 15-20 minutes.

**2** If some liquid remains, drain it away or serve a wetter quinoa. To finish, fold in the snow peas and carrot julienne. Adjust the seasoning before serving.

# SNOW PEAS AND CARROT JULIENNE

*Serves 4-6*
*Preparation and cooking.*

· **3 tablespoons salt**
· **4 cups (700g) snow peas**
· **ice cubes, for chilling**
· **4 tablespoons (50g) unsalted butter**
· **4 good-sized carrots, peeled,**
**quartered, then cut into matchsticks**
· **salt and pepper**

**1** In a saucepan, bring 4 cups (1l) water to a boil with 1 tablespoon salt. Add the snow peas and blanch for 2 minutes in the boiling water. Strain. Tip into a large bowl of chilled water. Strain again.

**2** Heat a sauté pan, melt three-quarters of the butter over medium-high heat. Tip the carrots into the bubbling butter, spread in well, season lightly. Stir for 2 minutes. Tip the carrots on to a plate and reserve while you finish cooking the snow peas.

**3** Return the pan to medium-high heat and add the rest of the butter. Spread in the snow peas, stir for 2 minutes, and take off the heat. Adjust the seasoning before serving.

# CHOCOLATE TRUFFLES

*with lavender and framboise*

*Makes about 1 lb (450g).
Preparation and cooking 1 hour,
freezing 3-4 hours.*

· **8 pieces diced fresh mango**
· **¼ lb (125g) high-quality bitter-
sweet chocolate**
· **¼ lb (125g) high-quality
milk chocolate**
· **1½ cups (350ml) heavy cream**
· **2 teaspoons dried lavender,
sealed in a tea ball or cheese cloth**
· **1½ sticks (175g) unsalted butter**
· **1 tablespoon framboise or Grand
Marnier (or other liqueur)**
· **2 ounces (60g) high-quality
unsweetened powdered cocoa**

**WINE SUGGESTIONS:**

Au Bon Climate Pinot Noir, Santa
Barbara or an Oregon white, Rex Hill
Pinot Gris.

**Turn your hand at being a chocolatier for a few hours and prepare these St. B truffles to give to friends. They are simply delicious. All you need is top-quality chocolate and powdered cocoa, a little time, and this recipe.**

**1** Break the two chocolates into small, even-sized pieces. Put in the small pan of a double boiler or in a bowl, which fits over a small saucepan. Put water in the bottom of the double boiler or in the saucepan, and bring to simmer. Place the pan/bowl with the chocolate on top. As soon as the chocolate starts to melt, stir with a wooden spoon until fully melted. Remove from heat, cover, and set aside.

**2** Put the cream in a small saucepan and place over low to medium heat. Add the sealed-in lavender. Bring to bubbling point. Immediately reduce the heat to minimum and lift out the lavender using a slotted spoon or tongs.

**3** Stir the chocolate into the pan a little at a time until blended in. Cut the butter into 6 pieces, whisk in a piece at a time. Mix in each piece completely before you add the next one. Once you've incorporated all the butter, stir in the framboise or Grand Marnier. Take off the heat. Place enough plastic wrap in a small bread pan to cover the inside completely and overlap generously all around the outside. Pour in the chocolate mixture, leave to cool to just above room temperature. Freeze for 3-4 hours.

**4** Take the pan out of the freezer, lift out the chocolate-filled wrap. Open the wrap over a cold work surface, cut the chocolate into neat ¾-1 inch (2-2.5cm) squares. Tip the powdered cocoa into a small bowl. Gently roll the squares into balls with the palm of your hand, then dip in the cocoa to coat all over.

**5** Place the truffles side by side, with a little space in between, in a single layer in a sealable container. Cover and refrigerate until ready to serve. The truffles will keep for up to a week in the refrigerator.

# MEET THE CHEFS

**Yann Yven:** Yann comes from Brittany, like Jean's mother, who taught him a few cooking tricks in his early days at the St. B, where he found himself at the start of a proposed long trip down to South America. He soon showed a great talent for cooking and a gift for making exquisite desserts. A well-traveled perfectionist, he can be trusted to maintain high standards and coolly resolve any culinary problems. Yann prefers to use organic produce and cook it healthily. His dishes are prepared and timed with rigorous precision, to respect the textures of ingredients and let their flavors come through. When not in the St. B Kitchen, Yann lives near the Rio Grande in a wonderful earthship house with his wife Pamela and their two children.

**Christopher Kelly White:** Chris is a born-and-bred Taoseño. He started working at the hotel carrying guests' luggage on Saturdays and doing the dishes during school vacations. After high school, Chris put on his first chef's jacket cooking on the deck. He worked there for a few years, dreaming of more challenging kitchen work. A source of inspiration was Taos's celebrated Joseph's Table. Jean sent him to the ICE chef's school in New York and he came back top of his class. He is now inspiring future chefs, teaching at the University of New Mexico in Taos, as well as cooking at the St. B where everyone is grateful to him for daily freshly baked bread.

**Randy Stabler:** Randall Laird Stabler believes that if you take care of the details the whole will take care of itself. Inspired by a 1920's child's cookbook, he started cooking as a kid. His relationship with the St. B kitchen goes back to the early '70s, when his duties involved *la plonge*, the washing up–giving him plenty of time on the slopes. He spent several years working and learning alongside Claude Gohard, left the St. B to work in California and the Far East, did a stint as a chef in the green zone in Baghdad, and keeps on coming back to the St. B kitchen because it's a happy place, where the work is varied. He looks after food orders and stock control.

...

**Patrick Yu:** (Previous page, on the right side) A Parisian with a Vietnamese father, Patrick is another person who succumbed to Ski Valley's charms. He first visited in '88, worked as a ski instructor and did various jobs in the kitchen. Having worked in Santa Fe as a restaurant manager, he came back 'for good' in 2005, and loves working as a chef in this most democratic kitchen. The combination of classic values and disciplined individuality suits his cooking style, as do the quality and variety of local ingredients. He is the resident expert on vegetables, which he loves to cook, often matching them with subtle spicing.

**Cindie White:** Having moved from Cape Cod to Los Alamos with her mother, Cindie came up to Taos to ski over twenty years ago. This is when she met Steve. Once 'caught in the port of entry', she made her life here. Brought up in an old New England inn and restaurant, she makes a mean Boston cream pie and very good pastries. She is totally at home cooking breakfast and lunch at the St. B; you could call it *en famille* with her husband Steve.

**Steve White:** Steve White describes his younger self with succinct modesty as a ski bum who liked cooking. Once upon a time in the South West... Legend has it that he and Jean met on a trail on horseback in the pouring rain. Steve still skis superlatively well. He once owned the restaurant at Lady Brett's house in Taos. One of the jobs he likes in the kitchen–where he takes care of breakfast and lunch–is baking, a talent he has passed on to his son Chris. He is also a talented musician, and an accomplished carpenter and builder. This last set of skills is put to good use in the summer months, repairing the inevitable toll the winter climates takes on the fabric of the St. B buildings.

# CLAUDE GOHARD: JEAN'S MOST TRUSTED ADVISER

There is a second kitchen dedicated to prepping food for the deck and the Rathskeller gourmet express bar. It's known as Claude's Kitchen, a little space of the St. B that will forever be his, despite the fact that he is now, in theory, enjoying retirement. Jean describes him as the soul of the St. Bernard kitchen and his most trusted adviser. Other former chefs who have influenced him are Yvon Silvé and Isao Kozaka. Claude has remained near Taos and comes up regularly, always willing to lend a hand and to make his signature Bœuf bourguignon or his ever popular Chili con carne. After a very tough childhood in war-torn France, Claude managed to become a classically trained chef de cuisine, a cook at the George V in Paris, to get the travel bug, work in Japan and on the West Coast, before finding himself in Taos, working with Jean on the beginnings of the inimitable repertoire of dishes.

# MONDAY

## THE WEEK GETS GOING

"Today really is the proper beginning of the ski week. If people need it, there's another ski-off on offer. We don't want anyone to feel stuck and unhappy in their ski group. It's important for people to know they have another opportunity to be placed in a class they feel compatible with, it's reassuring. Today's a chance to regroup. No fuss. As far as menus go, at lunch the soup is followed by carbohydrates—pasta or gnocchi—to give people energy for skiing in the afternoon. Dinner is very French: vegetable and bean soup with basil and garlic, roast Colorado lamb with a gratin, ratatouille, and upside-down apple tart—all very mouthwatering. Parts of the menu may be new to some of our guests. To be honest, I like trying to get people to try new foods that maybe they wouldn't have at home! They just need a little encouragement. But obviously, if there's something they can't eat, a special diet or an allergy, they just have to tell us and we'll do something special for them. Chef Chris is an ace at special requests."

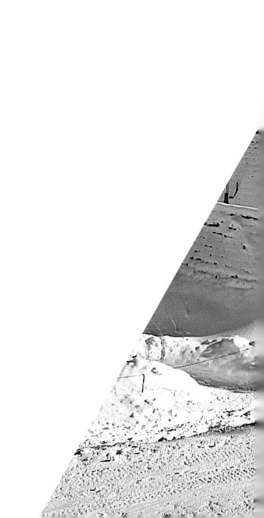

# CRANBERRY & BANANA BREAD

*Cindie's fruit breads*

*Makes 1 loaf.*
*Preparation, cooking and*
*cooling, 1½ hours.*

· **¼ cup (60ml) vegetable oil, plus**
**extra for greasing**
· **1½ cups (225g) all-purpose**
**flour, plus extra for flouring**
· **¾ teaspoon ground cinnamon**
· **½ teaspoon baking soda**
· **¼ teaspoon salt**
· **¼ teaspoon freshly grated nutmeg**
· **2 free-range medium eggs, beaten**
· **1 cup (225g) sugar**
· **2 teaspoons finely shredded**
**orange peel**
· **1 cup (250g) mashed ripe banana**
· **1 cup (125g) coarsely chopped**
**cranberries, fresh or frozen**

**You don't really need to have a sweet tooth to enjoy a slice of moist freshly baked fruity bread. Cindie's recipes are quick and simple. They're just as good later in the day with a cup of tea as they are for breakfast or brunch.**

**1** Preheat the oven to 350ºF (180ºC, mark 4). Grease and flour a 9 in (23 cm) loaf pan. In a bowl, mix together the flour, cinnamon, baking soda, salt, and nutmeg. Set aside.

**2** In a mixing bowl, combine the eggs, sugar, orange zest, banana, cranberries, and vegetable oil, until thoroughly mixed. Add the dry ingredients to the bowl, mix again until combined.

**3** Put in the prepared pan and bake for 50-60 minutes, until the center is just done and no longer sticky when you test it by inserting a metal skewer. Place the pan on a wire rack and leave to cool for 10 minutes before removing the bread from the pan.

# NUTTY GRANNY SMITH APPLE BREAD

*Cindie's fruit breads*

*Makes 12 portions.*
*Preparation, cooking, and cool-*
*ing, 1½ hours.*

· **½ cup (125g) margarine, plus**
**extra for greasing**
· *1* **free-range medium egg**
· *1* **cup (225g) sugar**
· *2* **cups (300g) flour, plus extra**
**for flouring**
· **pinch cinnamon**
· *1* **teaspoon baking soda**
· **½ cup (120ml) milk**
· *2* **cups (325g) peeled, cored and**
**chopped Granny Smith apples**
· **¼ cup (30g) chopped nuts (pecan**
**or walnuts or hazelnuts)**

**1** Preheat the oven to 350ºF (180ºC, gas 4). Grease and flour two 8 ½x4 ½x 2½in (21x11x6cm) pans.

**2** In a mixing bowl, cream the margarine, then beat in the egg, followed by the sugar. In another bowl, combine the flour, cinnamon, and baking soda.

**3** Now stir a third of the milk into the margarine mixture, followed by a third of the flour, then a third of the apples and nuts. Stir in well, but do not over-mix. Continue adding the rest of the ingredients in the same way, stirring well after each addition.

**4** Pour into the prepared pans and bake for 1 hour, or until the centers are just done and no longer sticky when tested with a metal skewer.

**5** Place the pans on a wire rack and leave to cool for 10 minutes before removing from the pan.

# PUY LENTIL SOUP

*with a dash of lime*

*Serves 4.*
*Preparation and cooking*
*30 minutes.*

· *2 scallions, chopped*
· **1 clove garlic, crushed**
· **1½ tablespoon olive oil**
· **1 qt (1l) chicken or vegetable stock (can be made from good concentrate)**
· **2-3 sprigs fresh thyme or 1 teaspoon dried thyme**
· **2 cups (400g) dark green lentils, rinsed**
· **salt and pepper**
· **grated zest and juice of 1 lime**

**To finish:**
· **piece of chilled butter (optional)**

Small dark, greeny-blue Puy lentils from the Auvergne region of France have a nutty texture and are less bland and floury than their larger paler relatives. If you can't find the real thing, a very similar variety is cultivated in Canada. Lime gives a distinctive St. B twist to this healthy fresh-tasting soup.

**1** Sauté the scallion and garlic in the oil in a heavy saucepan for 2-3 minutes until softened. Pour in the stock, add the thyme, and bring to a simmer over medium heat.

**2** Add the lentils and season lightly. Return to a simmer, cover, reduce the heat a little, and cook for 20-25 minutes, until the lentils are very soft.

**3** Turn off the heat and leave to cool for several minutes. Transfer half the soup to a blender or food processor and whiz until just smooth.

**4** Pour back into the saucepan. Stir in the lime zest and juice. Reheat gently, and taste and adjust the seasoning. Serve very hot. If you like, stir in a little chilled butter at the last minute.

**StB. tip:** For a luxe version of this soup, add a chopped celery stalk and a cup of diced carrots before your pour in the stock, simmer a little longer and finish off with a dollop of heavy cream or sour cream and chopped chives.

# SOUPE AU PISTOU

*with vegetables and radish sprouts*

*Serves 6-8.*
*Preparation and cooking 2 hours.*

· *1 tablespoon (15g) butter*
· *1 tablespoon olive oil*
· *1 large Vidalia onion, chopped*
· *salt and pepper*
· *2-3 carrots, diced*
· *2 stalks celery, chopped*
· *2 tablespoons dried Mediterra-nean herbs or herbes de Provence*
· *4 heaped tablespoons tomato paste*
· *3-4 cloves garlic, smashed*
· *6 oz (150g) tomatoes, chopped*
· *1 cup (240ml) red wine*
· *8 cups (2l) vegetable, chicken or beef stock*
· *3 cups (700g) mixed beans: pinto, kidney, lima, garbanzo, white, rinsed and pre-soaked*
· *2 bay leaves, fresh or dried*

**To garnish:**
· **handful radish tops, rinsed, drained, and chopped**

**For serving:**
· **Pistou (see opposite)**

**Chef Patrick is enthusiastic about this classic Provence vegetable and bean soup. It's well rounded, comforting, and has a heartiness that is very appropriate for winter fare. Ok, beans have a certain blandness, but it is more than well matched by lively Mediterranean flavors.**

**1** In a large heavy pot, melt the butter over medium heat. Add the oil, heat until sizzling, tip in the onion, and season lightly with salt and pepper.

**2** Stir the onion and cook until brown and beginning to caramelize. Add the carrots, celery, and a pinch of the herbs. Add the tomato paste, and stir for a few minutes until colored.

**3** Tip in the garlic, tomatoes, and wine, stir well, and cook until reduced, stirring several times. Pour in the stock and stir well. Take off the heat.

**4** Blend the mixture in a blender or food processor, and return to the pot; alternatively use a hand blender. Add the beans, bay leaves, and the rest of the herbs. Season to taste. Cover, return to low-medium heat, and simmer gently until the beans are soft but not mushy.

**5** Just before serving, scatter over radish tops. Serve with pistou.

# PISTOU

*Makes 1 cup (240ml).*
*Preparation and cooking*
*20 minutes.*

· **4 cloves garlic, smashed**
· **coarse sea salt**
· **leaves of** *2* **large handfuls basil**
· **½ cup (120ml) olive oil**
· *2-3* **tablespoons grated cheese**
**(Gruyère, Parmesan, Dry Jack or a**
**sharp Vermont Cheddar)**
· **pepper**

**Provence's version of pesto is traditionally made by pounding the ingredients using a pestle and mortar. Stir this zingy basil and garlic salsa into soups, pasta or rice just before serving. It also makes a good dip or a topping for croutons.**

**1** Put the garlic in the mortar with a little coarse sea salt. Pound with the pestle until crushed. Tear up half the basil, add to the mortar with a little more salt. Stir in and pound until mixed in. Add the rest of the basil and continue pounding until you have a thick mushy mixture. If you don't have a pestle and mortar, pulse the ingredients in the food processor taking care not to over-blend.

**2** Add the olive oil a little at a time, stirring and pounding (or pulsing in the food processor) until loosened into a thick sauce.

**2** Stir in the grated cheese. Season to taste with pepper.

# RACK OF TENDER COLORADO LAMB PROVENÇALE

*Serves 6-8.*
*Bringing the lamb to room*
*temperature, then preparation*
*and cooking 2 hours.*

· **3 french-cut racks lamb, trimmed**
**and ready to roast**
· *2* **teaspoons sea salt**
· *1* **teaspoon pepper**
· **¼ cup (60ml) clarified butter**
**(see St. B tip page 42)**
· **¼ cup (60ml) olive oil**
· **¼ cup (60ml) grapeseed oil**
· *7-8* **cloves garlic, crushed**
· *1* **medium onion, chopped**
· **½ cup (120ml) red wine**
· **6 oz (180ml) beer (½ can)**
**¼ cup Dijon mustard**
· *1* **tablespoon chopped fresh**
**parsley leaves**
· *2* **teaspoons Hungarian paprika**
· *3* **teaspoons plucked fresh**
**thyme leaves**
· *2* **teaspoons plucked fresh**
**rosemary leaves**
· *2* **tablespoons Champagne**
**or white wine vinegar**

**Top-quality meat needs to be treated with the TLC it deserves. Lean and luscious lamb from Colorado is a perfect meat for slow roasting. The St. B. method allows the meat to stay juicy and very pink while absorbing the flavors of the aromatic base.**

**1** Season the meat with salt and pepper. Bring the lamb to room temperature (allow 2 hours or so).

**2** Preheat the oven to cool, 220ºF (100ºC, gas ¼).

**3** Heat the butter and olive oil in large frying pan over medium-high heat. Place the racks top sides down in the pan to sear, and then also sear the meat with the rack bones pointing up. Remove from the heat. Put in a roasting pan with the bones facing down.

**4** In another frying pan, heat the grapeseed oil over medium-high heat and sauté the garlic and onion for 3-4 minutes. Pour in the wine and stir until bubbling to deglaze. Remove from the heat, stir in the beer, mustard, parsley, paprika, thyme, rosemary, and vinegar.

**5** Lift the racks from the roasting pan and spread them in the sautéed mixture, meat sides down. Cover the pan and put in the oven for 2-2 ½ hours. Check with meat thermometer: the internal temperature should read 140-145ºF (60-63ºC) for rare to medium-rare. Alternatively, cut about 2.5cm (1in) into the center of the rack: if red fluid runs out, the rack is done. Turn off the oven.

**6** Return the racks to the oven, uncovered, with the door closed. Leave to rest for at least 30 minutes before serving. Racks may rest up to 1 hour.

Jean and Dadou Mayer

# RATATOUILLE NIÇOISE

*Serves 6.*
*Preparation and cooking*
*1½ hours.*

**For the tomato base :**
· *3 tablespoons butter or oil*
· *1 onion, very thinly sliced*
· *1 teaspoon oregano*
· *1 tablespoon fresh chopped thyme*
**leaves or** *1 teaspoon dried thyme*
· *2 tablespoons tomato paste*
· *¾ cup (180ml) dry red wine*
· *2 cups (600g) crushed tomatoes*
· **salt and pepper**

**For the vegetables:**
· *1 cup (240ml) mild-flavored olive*
**oil, or a little more, for sautéing**
· *2 yellow squashes, cut into ¼ in.*
**(5mm) slices or half slices**
· **salt and pepper**
· *2 green zucchini cut into ¼ in.*
**(5mm) slices or half slices**
· *5 cups (550g) eggplant, cut into*
**¾ in. (2cm) dice**
· *3 cloves garlic, thinly sliced*
· *½ bell pepper, red or green, cut*
**into matchsticks**
· **tomato base (see above)**
· *½ cup (8 tablespoons) chopped*
**fresh basil**

**This great vegetable melting pot of Provence can be the best or the worst of dishes. At its worst it's a dull, soggy, oily stew; at its best a colorful aromatic confit of tender vegetables. The St. B version is as good as it gets, and inspired by Jean's brother Dadou Mayer. A stickler for perfection when it comes to favorite dishes, Dadou earned himself the nickname of 'Ratatouille Inspector'. Cinephile gourmets might like to know that Ratatouille is also a charming cartoon with Peter O'Toole as the voice of the restaurant critic A.N. Ego.**

**For the tomato base:**
**1** Put the oil or butter in a heavy pot. Over a medium-low heat, sauté the onion until golden brown. Add the oregano, thyme, and tomato paste, cook until brownish-red, stirring frequently. Add the wine and stir until bubbling, scraping the sides and bottom of the pot. Tip in the tomatoes, season lightly, stir, reduce the heat to low, simmer for 15 minutes, stirring now and then. Reserve.

**For the vegetables:**
**2** Preheat the oven to 350ºF (180ºC, gas mark 4). Pour in just enough oil to coat the bottom of a 10-12in (25-30cm) sauté pan. Place on a medium-high heat. Spread in some of the squash slices, making sure not to overcrowd the pan. Lightly season. Cook to golden brown each side. Lift out on to a plate lined with kitchen paper to drain off excess oil. Repeat in this way until you have cooked all the vegetables, cooking the garlic with the eggplant. If you like, use 2 sauté pans to speed up cooking.

**3** Once drained, put all the vegetables in a large roasting pan or casserole dish. Spoon the reserved tomato base over the vegetables, scatter over the basil and gently fold in once or twice. Loosely cover with parchment. Put in the oven for 30 minutes. Leave to cool a little before serving.

**St. B tip:** You can reserve the bell pepper matchsticks as a garnish. It will save you a little time and give a fresh finish to the ratatouille.

# PATRICK'S GRATIN DAUPHINOIS

*Serves 8.*
*Preparation and cooking 1 ¼ hours.*

· *8* medium Idaho or russet potatoes, peeled, kept in a bowl of cold water
· *1* qt (1l) milk
· salt and pepper
· 2 teaspoons (25g) butter
· *1* garlic clove, halved (optional)
· *3* cups (725ml) light or heavy cream
· good pinch freshly grated nutmeg
· *6* cups (700g) Gruyère cheese, grated

**Scalloped potatoes, tangy cheese, lush cream... this is comfort food at its best for a winter night, and a wonderful accompaniment for roasts – lamb, beef, venison, elk and duck breasts. This is Patrick's variation of the great gratin. At the St. B, Swiss Gruyère tends to be the favored cheese, but Alpenzeller, Reblochon, Roquefort, Stilton or occasionally Cheddar are also used. A hint of garlic and a touch of nutmeg round out the flavors.**

**1** Preheat the oven to 375ºF (190ºC, gas mark 5). Slice the potatoes very thinly. Put in a large pot with the milk and about the same amount of water—you need an extra 1in/2.5 cm of liquid above the potatoes. Season with a pinch of salt and bring to a boil. Bubble for 10 minutes. Take off the heat and drain well.

**2** While the potatoes are boiling, grease a baking dish with the butter and rub with the cut sides of the garlic, if you like. In a small pan, heat the cream until very hot. Take off the heat.

**3** Spread a layer of potatoes in the dish, season lightly with salt, pepper, and nutmeg, and scatter over one-third of the cheese. Cover with the remaining potatoes, season again with salt, pepper, and nutmeg. Pour over the hot cream.

**4** Bake until bubbling. Turn off the heat and leave to rest in the oven for about 15 minutes with the door closed (longer if convenient). Sprinkle the rest of the cheese over the dish. Broil for a few minutes for color. Serve hot.

# RANDY'S FRESH RADICCHIO SALAD

*Serves 6-8.*
*Preparation 20 minutes, resting time 1 ½ hours.*

· **1½ pounds (700g) fresh radicchio**
· **½ pound (225g) butter lettuce**

**For the lemon dressing:**
· **juice of *1* lemon**
· ***1* shallot, finely chopped**
· ***1-2* cloves garlic, crushed**
· **¼ cup (60ml) soy or tamari sauce**
· **1 tablespoon rice vinegar**
· **1 tablespoon finely chopped parsley**
· **¼ teaspoon ground coriander**
· **½ teaspoon salt**
· **¼ teaspoon pepper**
· **1 teaspoon sesame oil**
· **1 cup (240ml) grapeseed oil or olive oil**

**Randy's recipe combines bitter red radicchio and sweet tender lettuce with a sharp Oriental dressing. This is a very refreshing salad—ideal for serving alongside substantial winter dishes.**

**1** Start preparing this salad at least 1½ hours before you want to serve. Trim the leaves from the heads of salad, rinse in cold water. Dry in a salad spinner or pat with paper towels until dry.

**2** Reserving the oils, mix the other ingredients for the lemon dressing in a bowl, leave for at least ½ hour to allow flavors to blend.

**3** Whisk the oils together until blended. Drizzle into the bowl, whisking vigorously until the dressing emulsifies. Put the radicchio in a large shallow bowl, pour over ¾ of the dressing, and toss until coated. Set aside at room temperature for at least 1 hour. This softens the leaves and allows them to absorb the flavors of the dressing.

**2** At the last minute, toss in the butter lettuce, adding a little more dressing if needed.

# THE CALM BEFORE THE STORM

The dining room before dinner. Shining glasses and thick linen napkins, hospitable no-nonsense place mats and jugs of water, chilled butter, a mouthwatering menu, warm lighting, and a cozy, funky atmosphere... the tables are ready to welcome weary happy skiers. The scene is set for Jean to bring out the dishes, ably assisted by tonight's front of house team Erika, Pierre-André, Sacha, Krizia, and Leif.

# TARTE TATIN

*Serves 6-8.*
*Preparation, cooking, and*
*cooling 2½ hours.*

· *6 tablespoons (75g) butter*
· *½ cup (125g) sugar*
· *¼ cup (60ml) lemon juice*
· **1 tablespoon each arrowroot and cornstarch**
· *8 apples (Golden Delicious, Winsap or Gala) peeled, halved, and cored*
· *1 X brisée pastry dough*
**(see opposite)**

**For serving:**
· **Chantilly (see page 26)**

**Apple pie may be American, but tarte tatin is definitely French. Once upon a time in the little town of Lamotte-Beuvron, not far from Orléans, there were two sisters named Tatin who had a restaurant. They made a pretty good apple tart. One day there was an accident in the kitchen and the tart ended up being cooked upside down... Jean sometimes tells another version of the story and says that one of the sisters burnt the apples and covered them up with pastry. Whatever really happened, the glorious upside-down caramelized dessert was born. The St. B's recipe is top of the class.**

**1** Preheat the oven to 350°F (180°C, gas mark 4). In a bowl, combine the butter, sugar, lemon juice, arrowroot, and cornstarch. Add the apples, stir until coated. Arrange the apples, round sides down, in a flameproof roasting pan or ovenproof sauté pan. Pack them tightly together in concentric circles, starting on the outside.

**2** Bake for 45 minutes or until the juices turn amber. If you prefer, cook in the sauté pan covered with a lid on top of the stove on low-medium heat. Let cool in the pan to room temperature. Take the Brisée dough out of the refrigerator, roll it out into a shape slightly larger than the pan and ¼ in (6-7mm) thick.

**3** Place the dough on top of the apples, trimming the edges and tucking the sides down between the apples and the pan. Bake for 40-45 minutes, or until golden brown.

**4** Let cool to room temperature. Loosen the edges with a knife. Place the pan on the stovetop on medium high heat for 2-3 minutes. This will loosen the sugars attaching the tart to the pan and dry off excess moisture.

**5** Once the tart moves freely when you shift the pan back and forth gently, cover the pan with a slightly larger serving plate. Using oven mitts and holding the plate and pan together, turn everything over so that the tart sits on the plate with the apples on top. Gently lift off the pan.

**6** Serve warm with Chantilly.

# BRISÉE PASTRY DOUGH

*Makes about ½ pound (225g).*
*Preparation and chilling*
*45 minutes.*

- *1 cup (150g) unbleached flour*
- *½ cup (50g) cake flour*
- *¼ teaspoon salt*
- *⅛ teaspoon baking powder*
- *1 stick (125g) butter, cut into 1 in.*
(2.5cm) pieces
- *2 tablespoons apple cider vinegar*
- *¼ cup (60ml) ice water plus*
extra if needed

**WINE SUGGESTIONS:**
Château La Bastide Dauzac, Margaux.

**1** Make the dough: In a mixing bowl, combine the flours, salt, and baking powder. Rub in the butter pieces either by hand or with the paddle of an electric mixer on lowest speed, until the mixture resembles coarse crumbs.

**2** Stir the apple cider vinegar into the ice water. Sprinkle over the mixture and work in until the dough holds together. Gather the dough out of the bowl, and shape into a 3 in (7.5cm) circle. Wrap in plastic and chill for at least 30 minutes or until needed.

# TUESDAY

**CATCHING THE RHYTHM IN THE KITCHEN AND ON THE SLOPES...**

"The art of French cuisine is the art of accommodating food to whatever you have on hand and making it savory, healthy, and an experience of good taste. You don't have to be in France to cook à la française. You can cook in the French spirit wherever you are. Take Croque Madame... you could call it a nice grilled ham and cheese sandwich with a white cream cheese sauce and an egg on top. In France, you'd eat it for lunch, but here we serve it for breakfast. That's because in the US people are used to having a big breakfast. For me this dish brings back plenty of memories. When my parents had a restaurant in Nice at the end of the Second World War, American sailors were crazy about eating Croque Madame or Croque Monsieur, the same thing but without the egg. After a while it became quite a tradition. Another great tradition of the St. B is today's dinner, our famous paella, made to measure to please as many of our guests as possible, while remaining authentic. The preparation goes on evolving in order to respond to the wishes of the guests who are here for the week. If a dish challenges the chefs' creativity, this is it... But I have a feeling they're quite happy about it."

# CROQUE MADAME

*Serves 4.*
*Preparation and cooking*
*20 minutes.*

· 4 slices French country bread or other good bread
· soft unsalted butter for spreading and for cooking the eggs
· 4 slices good smoked ham, jambon de Paris or good Virginia ham
· 4 slices Gruyère cheese
· béchamel sauce (see following recipe)
· 4 free range eggs
· salt and pepper
· paprika and cayenne

When Jean prepares a croque ham sandwich, he likes to put butter on the bread; 'It tastes better that way. I also find it's best without another piece of bread on the top, which some people prefer!' This chic grilled sandwich can be served with a garnish of green salad and a slice of cantaloupe.

**1** Preheat the broiler. Very lightly toast the bread. Put the slices on a platter, spread with butter. Place a slice of ham on the bread, then top with a slice of cheese. Spread over some Béchamel sauce. Set aside.

**2** Put some butter in a frying pan, cook the eggs sunny side up. Using a slotted spoon or a fish slice, put an egg on top of each sandwich. Season with a little salt, pepper, paprika and cayenne. Put under the broiler for a couple of minutes and serve immediately.

# BÉCHAMEL SAUCE

*Makes about 1 ½ cups (350ml).*
*Preparation and cooking*
*30 minutes.*

· 2 tablespoons butter (30g)
· 2 heaped tablespoons flour
· 1 cup milk (240ml)
· salt and pepper
· tiny pinch nutmeg
· tiny pinch paprika
· 3 tablespoons heavy cream
· 4 tablespoons grated Gruyère or sharp Cheddar cheese

A smooth luxe version of the mother of French white sauces, enriched with cream and cheese. Double the quantities and use to dress pasta, broccoli, or cauliflower.

**1** Heat the butter in a heavy-bottomed saucepan over medium heat. Whisk in the flour, and cook for 1-2 minutes, until it turns a light blond color.

**2** Tip in the milk and whisk steadily until it comes to a boil. Reduce heat to very low, season lightly with salt, pepper, nutmeg, and paprika. Stir in the cream and simmer for another 15 minutes.

**2** Stir in the grated cheese until it is completely melted.

# GREEN CHILI STEW

*Serves 4-6.*
*Preparation and cooking 1 ½ hours.*

· *1 tablespoon olive oil*
· *¾ pound (350g) pork tenderloin (or chicken fillet), cut ½ in (1.5 cm) pieces*
· *1 large onion, finely chopped*
· *3 cloves garlic, crushed*
· *1 ½ pounds (700g) fire roasted mild New Mexican green chiles, such as Anaheim, peeled, seeded, and finely chopped*
· *2 teaspoons-2 tablespoons Jalapeños, finely diced (can be fresh, canned or frozen and defrosted)*
· *1 teaspoon cumin*
· *1 teaspoon dried oregano*
· *4 cups (1l) vegetable or chicken stock, plus extra if needed*
· *1 large russet potato, cut into small chunks*
· *½ cup (200g) crushed tomatoes*
· *salt and pepper*

**New Mexican Chili Verde stew tends not to feature tomatoes, but a little tomato is included here to round off the flavors. Use jalapeños to add heat to the mild green chiles. This is just as good reheated and also freezes well.**

**1** In a heavy-bottomed pot, heat the oil on medium-high heat. Sauté the meat for about 5 minute, then move it to the sides of the pot. Add the onion and garlic, and sauté and stir with the meat as soon as the mixture colors a little.

**2** Stir in the chiles, cumin, oregano, and the stock. Bring to a simmer, and add the potato and tomatoes. Reduce the heat to very low, cover, and simmer for 1 hour or until tender. Stir from time to time, and add a little stock if necessary. Adjust the seasoning before serving.

**St. B tip:** If roasted Anaheim or other New Mexican green chiles are not available, use a grill or griddle pan to roast chiles until black all over. Put in a plastic bag, freeze for 10 minutes. Rub off the blackened peel, rinse, halve lengthwise, seed, and finely chop.

▲

# SPOON BREAD

*Serves 4-6.*
*Preparation and cooking 1 ½ hours.*

- ¼ **cup (50g) butter**
- ½ **cups (300g) chopped onion**
- ½ **cup (125g) fire-roasted mild green chiles, chopped**
- *1* **cup (240ml) sour cream**
- **pinch salt**
- *2* **cups (225g) shredded sharp Cheddar**
- *1* **egg, beaten**
- ½ **cup (120ml) milk**
- *1 x 8* **oz (225g) can cream style corn, drained**
- *1 x 10* **oz (275g) corn muffin mix (Jiffy)**
- **Pam spray**

**Freshly made, soft-textured spoon bread is perfect with a chili stew.**

**1** Preheat the oven to 425ºF (220ºC, gas mark 7). Melt the butter in a frying pan over medium heat, add the onion, and sauté gently until translucent and softened. Reduce the heat a little, add the chiles, and sauté for a couple of minutes without browning. Take off the heat, and let cool to room temperature.

**2** Stir in the sour cream and season lightly with salt. Stir in half the cheese and put aside.

**3** In a bowl, combine the egg, milk, corn, and muffin mix. Pam spray an 8 in (20cm) baking pan. Pour in the muffin mixture, knock on the worktop to smooth, and spoon the sour cream mixture evenly on top. Sprinkle with the rest of the cheese.

**4** Bake for 35 minutes. Leave to cool to room temperature before turning out.

# THE GREAT DECONSTRUCTED PAELLA VALENCIENNE

The St. B Paella is a genuine tour de force – a group effort for the chefs, who cook the components separately. The reason is that, while everybody loves to eat a great paella, many people are allergic to, or unable to eat, some of the ingredients–maybe seafood, shellfish, chicken, pork... So the solution is to deconstruct the dish and keep the various elements well apart. Guests end up creating their very own paella. It has to be said that paella night is not the evening for a novice to try dishing out the food at his or her table. Only safe and decisive pairs of hands need volunteer to serve. When you cook the St. B paella at home, read the recipes in detail (please), and pick what you and your guests like. You'll be able to put a class act of a dish on your table. And if the whole thing is too daunting, the individual recipes are delicious separately.

# PAELLA RICE AND NEW POTATO GARNISH

*Serves 6.*
*Preparation and cooking 1¼ hours.*

· *4-6* new potatoes (San Luis Valley purple potatoes if possible), quartered
· *4* tablespoons olive oil
· *2* Roma tomatoes, quartered
· salt and pepper
· *4* tablespoons (50g) butter
· *1* onion, finely chopped
· *2* carrots, finely chopped
· *1* clove garlic, crushed
· *1* teaspoon saffron strands
· *2–4* tablespoons red chile powder
· *1* tablespoon cumin (use more if going easy on red chile)
· good pinch oregano
· *2* cups (375g) rinsed brown rice
· *4-4½* cups (950ml-1.1 l) water
· *½* cup (60g) peas,
thawed if frozen

**Use long- or short-grain rice; always look at the instructions on the packaging. Don't forget to allow the steam to escape at the end of cooking the rice.**

**1** Preheat the oven to 350ºF (180ºC, gas mark 4).

**2** Put the potatoes in a roasting pan, drizzle with half the olive oil, stir, season, and roast for 45 minutes.

**3** When these go in the oven, put the tomatoes in a second roasting pan, drizzle with the rest of the olive oil, season and roast for 30 minutes. Reserve.

**4** Put a 2 quart (2l) pot which has a lid on medium-low heat and melt the butter in it. Tip in the onion and carrots, and cook until golden, stirring frequently. Add the garlic, and cook until it releases its aroma. Add the saffron, red chile, cumin, and oregano. Season lightly and stir for 1-2 minutes.

**5** Add the rice, stir for 3 minutes, add the water, and bring to a boil, stirring frequently. Reduce to a simmer, cover, and cook until just done – allow 45-55 minutes and follow cooking time on packaging.

**6** Once the rice is cooked, take off the heat and remove the lid to allow the steam to escape for 2 minutes. Add the roast tomatoes and the peas, and fork the rice gently. Cover and keep in a warm place if not using immediately.

**7** Serve alongside the potatoes and the other ingredients.

SHARON

TRACY

# CATERING FOR ALL PALATES

Each table has a number. If a guest has a specific request, it will be noted with his or her name near the table number. This is particularly important with a composite dish like paella. Over the years the St. B kitchen has become expert at vegetarian dishes, as well as vegan and gluten-free menu.

# SAFFRON CHICKEN & CHORIZO

*Serves 6.*
*Marinating 2 hours, then preparation and cooking 1¼ hours.*

· **2 tablespoons cumin**
· **1 tablespoon paprika**
· **2 teaspoons Thai chile powder**
· **1 tablespoons saffron**
· **½ cup olive oil**
· **juice 1 lemon**
· **juice 2 limes**
· **4 cloves garlic, slivered**
· **2 heaped tablespoons chopped fresh parsley**
· **6 whole chicken leg portions, skin on**
· **4 tablespoons grapeseed oil.**
· **⅛ cup (30ml) dry white wine.**
· **2 chorizo sausages**

**This recipe is scrumptiously easy and a great supper dish.**

**1** In a cup, mix together the cumin, paprika, chile powder, and saffron. In a mixing bowl, combine the olive oil, lemon and lime juices, garlic, and parsley. Stir in the dry spice mixture.

**2** Add the chicken pieces and gently toss in the mixture until coated, using a rubber spatula or your hands. Cover and refrigerate for 2 hours.

**3** Preheat the oven to 375ºF (190ºC, gas mark 5). Put the grapeseed oil in a sauté pan over medium heat. Lift the chicken pieces out of the marinade, reserving the marinade. Fry for 10 minutes each side until well seized and colored. Using tongs, transfer the chicken pieces to a deep baking pan.

**4** Turn up the heat under the sauté pan, and add the white wine and the marinade. Bubble for 2-3 minutes. Pour into the baking pan and put in the preheated oven.

**5** After 20 minutes, put the chorizo in the pan with the chicken or if you prefer in a separate oven pan. Cook with the chicken for 20 minutes.

**6** Cover the pans and reserve in a warm place until ready to use. Thickly slice the chorizo before serving.

# FRESH FISH AND SEAFOOD STEW

*Serves 6.*
*Preparation and cooking*
*30 minutes.*

· *3* **cups (720ml) fish fumet or**
**stock (see tip below)**
· **caramelized shallots (see recipe**
**page 100)**
· *12* **clams (fresh and scrubbed, or**
**frozen or cooked)**
· *12* **mussels (fresh and scrubbed,**
**or frozen or cooked)**
· **marinated squid (see recipe**
**page 100)**
· *1* **pound (450g) skinned and**
**boned fish pieces (cod, tuna,**
**snapper, haddock, salmon)**
· **¼ cup (4 tablespoons) chopped**
**fresh parsley**
· **pepper**

**The St. B team use a fondue pot to poach the fish and seafood in fumet. It's all too easy to overcook and spoil delicate textures so the stew is done separately and at the last minute. If using fresh clams and mussels, first wash and scrub them, then keep them covered with ice in a colander. If one of your guests doesn't like shellfish, poach these separately in a little fish fumet.**

**1** Put the fish fumet in a pan on medium-low heat. Bring to a simmer.

**2** A few minutes before serving, heat a large heavy pot, add the shallots, then the clams and mussels (if fresh) and the squid, Pour in the fish fumet. Stir, bring to a simmer, and add the fish. Stir and cook for 2 minutes. If the clams and mussels are already cooked, add them now with the parsley. Season with pepper and bring to simmer. Serve as soon as possible.

**St. B tip:** To make a quick fish fumet or stock, bring to a simmer 1 quart (1litre) Yann's white vegetable stock (page 19). Add 3 x 2 in (5cm) strips each lemon and orange zest, a tablespoon crushed dried fennel seeds, a cup dry white wine and a cup trimmings from white fish/shellfish. Return to a boil, reduce the heat, and simmer 15-20 minutes. Strain and leave to get cold before refrigerating or freezing.

# CARAMELIZED SHALLOTS

*Preparation and cooking*
*25 minutes.*

· *1½ tablespoons grape seed oil*
· *2 large shallots, finely minced*
· *1 tablespoon bourbon*
· *1 tablespoon (15g) butter*

**This short recipe is a winner–guaranteed to add a sweet, deep je-ne-sais-quoi to sauces, stews, and soup.**

**1** Put the oil in a small pan on medium heat. Add the shallots and sauté for 3-5 minutes until just golden.

**2** Remove the pan from the heat, and add the bourbon. Return to the heat, set alight and flambé. Reduce heat to low and cook gently for 10 minutes, stirring occasionally. Whisk in the butter to finish.

# MARINATED SQUID

*Serves 6.*
*Preparation and marinating*
*1-¼ hours.*

· *12 **pieces of squid (rings and tentacles), fresh or frozen***
· *2 **tablespoons olive oil***
· *1 **tablespoon dry lavender** or **rosemary***
· *1 **teaspoon pepper***
· *2 **lemon slices, chopped***
· *½ **clove garlic, crushed (optional)***
· *1 ½ **tablespoons white wine***

**This is a good way to prepare squid ahead of cooking. It adds flavor and softens their texture.**

**1** Rinse the squid with cold water and reserve. If you like, chop the larger pieces.

**2** In a small bowl, mix the remaining ingredients, then add the squid. Stir to coat, cover, and refrigerate for at least 1 hour or until ready to use.

# SAUTÉED SHRIMP

*with garlic & lemon butter*

*Serves 6.*
*Preparation and cooking*
*20 minutes.*

· *4 tablespoons (50g) butter*
· *12 large raw shrimp, cleaned and deveined*
· *1 clove garlic, crushed*
· *½ cup (120ml) lemon juice*
· *¼ cup (60ml) dry white wine*

**Chris's recipe is simplicity itself. The trick is to add the shrimp just after you've put in the garlic–you don't want the garlic to burn and turn acrid. If you cook the shrimp on their own, the recipe will serve 2-4. Add chopped fresh parsley or basil at the end.**

**1** Heat a pan on medium-high heat until very hot but not smoking. Melt the butter in it. Add the garlic to the melted butter and immediately tip in the shrimp – you don't want the garlic to burn.

**2** Swirl the shrimp in the garlic butter until they are pinkish orange and half-cooked.

**3** Add the lemon juice and the wine, and bring to a simmer. Reduce the heat, cover, and cook 3 minutes.

**Serving paella St. B style:** Take a big platter, put the rice in the center with the potatoes on top. The chicken and chorizo go on one side, the sautéed shrimp on the other. Put the seafood in a separate shallow bowl. What you now need, of course, is Jean bringing it all to the table with a big smile. But, failing that, drink a toast to absent friends.

# BELGIAN ENDIVE & TOMATO SALAD

*with shallot & lime vinaigrette*

*Serves 6.*
*Preparation 20 minutes.*

· **4 large Belgian endives**
· **2-3 beefsteak or Roma tomatoes**
· **10-12 cherry tomatoes**
· **shallot & lime vinaigrette (see opposite)**
· **½ cup (65g) chopped walnuts (optional)**

**Use endive leaves as a scoop for a perfect bite of this palate-cleansing salad. It's just as good served before a big entrée as it is afterwards.**

**1** Cut off the ends of the endives and remove the outer layer of leaves. Pull out the larger leaves, and finely mince the smaller ones and the heart. Slice the large tomatoes; chop the cherry tomatoes.

**2** In a large platter, fan out the endive leaves. Place the tomatoes on top in the center. Scatter over the minced endive. Drizzle over the vinaigrette and sprinkle over the walnuts, if using. Serve soon.

# SHALLOT & LIME VINAIGRETTE

*Makes 2 cups (480ml).*
*Preparation 20 minutes.*

· *1* cup (240ml) olive oil
· *½* cup (120ml) balsamic vinegar
· salt and pepper
· *¼* cup (50g) finely minced shallots
juice of *2* limes and/or lemons
· *1-2* tablespoons Dijon mustard
· *2* eggs
· *1* tablespoon finely minced fresh
tarragon or sorrel or *2* teaspoons
finely minced thyme leaves (optional)

There are as many variations on vinaigrette as your imagination permits. In Patrick's recipe, the shallots add a touch of tart sweetness that balances out the citrusy acidity. Add herbs if you like, but keep flavors clean and simple. Keep unused vinaigrette for up to 2 weeks in a sealed container in the refrigerator. Shake before using in salads, marinades, rubs, and even in some sauces.

1 Put the olive oil and vinegar in a glass or stainless steel bowl. Whisk in a pinch of salt and a little pepper. Add the shallots and lime/lemon juice. Whisk briefly, then whisk in the mustard.

2 Coddle the eggs: boil them for 2 minutes in boiling water, scoop out the yolks and discard the whites. Add the yolks to the dressing and whisk briefly.

3 Stir in the herbs, if using, and adjust the seasoning.

# PANNA COTTA

*Serves 6-8.*
*Preparation and cooking 40 minutes, cooling and chilling 6 hours or overnight.*

· ¼ oz (6g) leaf gelatin
(check packaging)
· ⅓ cup (80ml) buttermilk
· 2½ cups (600ml) heavy cream
· ½ cup (125g) fine baking sugar
· ½ teaspoon Madagascar vanilla extract or seeds and pulp from fresh pods
· 2 fresh kiwis, peeled and sliced

**For drizzling:**
· honey rose syrup (see following recipe)

**For serving:**
· almond butter cake
(see recipe page 111)

**Yann's recipe for a terrific Italian custard with a subtle texture is fun to make and looks very pretty on the plate. Of course, you can bake it in a single dish, but it's much more special and elegant served with a flourish on dessert plates. You can replace the kiwi with berries or nectarine.**

**1** Cut the gelatin in small pieces. Put in a glass bowl and add the buttermilk. Stir gently with a spatula until the gelatin is completely covered. Leave to soften at room temperature for 15 minutes or until needed.

**2** In a medium saucepan, stir together the cream and sugar. Put on medium heat and bring to a rolling boil, watching constantly as heavy cream will rise fast. Pour in the buttermilk and gelatin, and stir constantly for 2 minutes.

**3** Take off the heat and stir in the vanilla. Stir for 2-3 minutes. Pour into a pitcher, then from this into 6-8 individual ramekins. Leave the ramekins to cool to room temperature.

**4** Cover with plastic wrap and refrigerate for at least 5 hours, preferably overnight.

**5** Just before serving, have a deep 2in (5cm) pan 2/3 full of very hot water ready. Dip in the ramekins a few at a time for 6-10 seconds. Invert carefully onto dessert plates. Add a slice of kiwi, drizzle with Honey rose syrup and serve with a slice of almond butter cake.

# HONEY ROSE SYRUP

*Makes 1 cup (240ml).
Preparation and cooking 15
minutes, cooling 30 minutes.*

· **½ cup (120ml) honey**
· **½ cup (120ml) cold water**
· **pure rosewater in a spray bottle**

**Try and use local honey if available. You will find spray bottles of pure rosewater in herb stores – beware of the synthetic stuff.**

**1** In a small saucepan bring the honey and water to a gentle simmer on low heat, stirring a few times.

**2** Spray with rosewater a couple of times, then stir once or twice. Leave to simmer for 3 minutes. Take off the heat and let cool to room temperature before serving.

# ALMOND BUTTER CAKE

*Serves 6-8.*
*Preparation and baking 1hour*
*5 minutes, cooling 25 minutes.*

· *1½ sticks (190g) unsalted butter*
· *3 medium large fresh eggs*
· *⅔ cup (180g) fine sugar*
· *1½ cup (180g) baking flour*
· *1½ tablespoons almond flour*
· *pinch of salt*

**WINE SUGGESTION:**

Kistler Vine Hill Chardonnay, Sonoma.

**This lovely light cake is also very good served with poached, stewed, or roasted fruit. If you want, take out your kitchen scales before you start baking: you need the same weight each of shell-on eggs, sugar, butter, and combined flours. The quantities below are based on using eggs weighing 2 oz (60g) each.**

**1** Preheat the oven to 400ºF (200ºC, gas mark 6). Reserve 2 teaspoons of butter for greasing the pan, melt the rest in a small pan on low heat.

**2** Separate the eggs and reserve the whites in the refrigerator. Put the yolks and the sugar in the bowl of a mixer or food processor, beat on medium speed until pale and buttery looking. Add the melted butter at low speed.

**3** Reserve 1½ tablespoons flour for flouring the pan. Sift the rest into a bowl, and mix in the almond flour and salt. Stir into the egg and sugar mixture until blended in. Reserve in a warm place by the oven.

**4** In a clean bowl, whisk the egg whites until little peaks form. Fold gently into the mixture with a wooden spoon, working from the top to the bottom and always in the same direction, until smoothly mixed in.

**5** Grease a baking pan, add the reserved flour, shake well and tip out excess. Pour in the cake mixture and spread evenly. Knock against the work surface.

**6** Bake for 15 minutes, then reduce the heat to 350ºF (180ºC, gas mark 4) and bake for another 15 minutes. Take out of the oven. Turn out on to a cooling rack, and let cool for 25 minutes.

**7** The cake can be served still warm or at room temperature.

# BEHIND THE SCENES AT THE ST. B ?

Why the question mark? The simple answer is that there's not really such a thing as 'behind the scenes' at the St. Bernard... One of the great charms of the place is that what you see is what you get. 'Transparency' has become a buzzword, and a claim often made by all kinds of organizations, but it's a word that genuinely describes the running of the hotel.

This has something to do with size. Because it is small and compact, doors and corridors don't separate guests and staff. Truth be told, they keep on bumping into each other. What works so well and seamlessly is that there are boundaries under the informality, but not of the kind that is regulated by 'Staff Only' notices. Nobody on the team flattens himself or herself against the wall, pretending to be invisible, when a guest walks by. Everyone is smiling, friendly, helpful, happy to join in a chat when prompted–but don't expect obsequious 'madam'-ing. Take the housekeeping team... every morning as skiers stomp around on their way out, the team can be seen having breakfast at one end of the dining room before they whiz around making the rooms pristine again and discreetly restoring order. The Montoya family have been keeping the St.B. clean (and cheering up patron Jean, seen with his hand on the sadly much missed Frances Montoya's shoulder on the picture opposite taken a few years ago) for three generations.

More often than not, staff meetings at the hotel take the form of a team of people–front of house, kitchen, and housekeeping–having breakfast together to talk about things, with Jean dashing in and out and being just elusive enough to keep everyone on their toes.

Taoseños are nothing if not multi-talented. People choose to come and work at the St. B because they like it, rather like guests keep on coming back year after year. Andrea Heckman, has a PhD in Latin American Studies, runs her two Andean Software shops, leads travel tours and makes documentaries, yet still enjoys being a part-time member of the bar and front-of-house team, as well as taking to the dance floor at the end of her shift.

# KITCHEN TALK

*Patrick had a good idea for the shrimps... Please use a little less salt in soups, it's supposed to enhance flavor, not make a dish taste salty... let's try serving a larger crepe like Chris suggested... what about a touch of red wine vinegar in this sauce... where can we get great fresh radicchio?* Every year before the season starts, Jean and the chefs discuss menus and dishes. New recipes are tried, old favorites revisited. In his role as *chef d'orchestre*, Jean uses a pen rather than a baton, and starts off with written detailed notes about dishes and how to present them. There's no head chef at the St. B. This might come as a surprise, as it is very unconventional practice in the hotel and restaurant world, but it works extremely well here. It enables the six chefs to use their imagination while they cook the dishes for which they are responsible. At the same time as it encourages them to work creatively as individuals, it helps build team spirit (incidentally, for that matter, that's also how Jean encourages people to ski). Everybody has to be able to step in and help with a dish, or indeed cook it, when needed. Many dishes are team efforts, such as the paella served on Tuesday night. Jean may well be a very relaxed maestro, but he won't tolerate complicated food: what matters is the flavor, the taste of a dish, the way it looks when it is brought to the table. The flavor of an ingredient is never camouflaged nor changed, just enhanced. As a result of this approach, it is essential to buy best quality produce, fresh and local when possible. Suppliers are very much under scrutiny during the pre-season kitchen planning. Chefs must know where fish comes from, whether meat is grass-fed or properly aged. Do vegetables have an honest flavor? Are they as truly organic as advertised? Is this chile just hot or does it also have a nice flavor? Just as Jean is constantly in touch with the latest technical skiing trends and developments, he also keeps abreast of culinary developments –the St. B cuisine is always evolving to suit the changing palates and tastes of the guests. But what about budget? There is always also the added expense of getting supplies delivered all the way up to the hotel. The best product available isn't cheap, but Jean says–with just a hint of a twinkle–that he pays attention to costs by serving very slightly smaller portions. Gourmet guests yes, gluttons never...

# WEDNESDAY

**AN AFTERNOON OFF THE SLOPES**

"Time seems to be gathering speed and more than half the week is gone. Some skiers' aching muscles tell them they have exerted themselves. If people mention that they are skiing less well rather than better and that they are feeling tired, I encourage them to get off the mountain and drive down to Taos for the afternoon. They can walk around, relax and explore the art galleries. It's another world down there. Taos is an incredible melting pot of cultures: native Americans, Mexicans, Europeans, expats from the East Coast; the town has a very attractive heritage and a lot to offer. And the landscape is stunning. It can still take my breath away after all these years. Up on our mountains in the Ski Valley, it's hard to believe that nineteen miles down the road you have stunning vistas stretching on and on as far as the eye can see, the Rio Grande gorge and an all-enveloping and incredibly luminous sky."

# HUEVOS RANCHEROS

*Serves 4.*
*Preparation and cooking*
*20-30 minutes.*

· *4-6 tablespoons (50-75g)*
**butter for frying**
· *½ 16 oz (400g) can black beans,*
**drained, rinsed, and drained again**
· **4 small corn tortillas**
· **4 free-range eggs**
· **salt and pepper**
· **green chile sauce, gently heated**
**(see page 120)**
· *1 cup (125g) grated Cheddar cheese*
· *2 Roma tomatoes, peeled,*
**seeded, and diced**
· *2 tablespoons shredded*
**butter lettuce**
· *1 tablespoon chopped cilantro*

**Continuing the St. B's international parade of great breakfast egg dishes comes a hot favorite from Mexico. It's just as good if you make it with scrambled eggs: what matters is the combination of soft egg, tortilla, beans, and chile salsa.**

**1** In a saucepan on low-medium heat, melt a tablespoon (15g) butter. Add the beans and cook gently until hot, stirring now and then. Keep hot.

**2** Melt another tablespoon (15g) butter in a frying pan on medium-high heat. Fry the tortillas and place on warmed plates (you might need to add a little butter between the tortillas). Keep warm.

**3** Add a tablespoon (15g) more butter to the frying pan. Crack the eggs into the skillet and cook for 3-4 minutes for runny yolks, a little longer if you prefer them firmer. Season lightly.

**4** To serve, spoon the beans on the tortillas, add the eggs, then spoon over some green chile sauce. Top with grated cheese, diced tomato, shredded lettuce, and chopped cilantro.

**St.B tip:** To peel tomatoes, score a cross on top, opposite the stalk end. Drop into a pot of boiling water (a bowl of just-boiled water will do) for 1-2 minutes, depending on size. Lift out with a slotted spoon, drain. Once cool enough to handle, slip off the skin. To seed, halve the tomatoes and squeeze out the pulp and seeds over a bowl (with a sieve on top for the juice).

# GREEN CHILE SAUCE

*Makes 3 cups (720ml). Preparation and cooking 1½ hours.*

· *2 tablespoons olive oil*
· *1 cup (175g) chopped fire-roasted mild green chile*
· *1 cup (175g) chopped fire-roasted hot green chile*
· *6 garlic cloves, crushed*
· *1 medium onion, diced*
· *4 tablespoons dried oregano*
· *pinch ground cumin*

**The New Mexican cook's little helper; this is a very good sauce to have at hand in the kitchen.**

**1** Heat the oil in a heavy saucepan on low–to–medium heat. Stir in the chiles, garlic, and onion. Add 2 cups hot water, stir. Cook for about 40 minutes until softened, stirring from time to time.

**2** Stir in the oregano and cumin. Take off the heat and leave to get cold, stirring a few times to mix thoroughly. Cover and refrigerate – the sauce will keep for several days.

# FRESH CORN CHOWDER

*Serves 6-8.*
*Preparation and cooking 2 hours.*

- *1 tablespoon (15g) butter*
- *1 tablespoon olive oil*
- *1 large Vidalia onion, chopped*
- *1 carrot, chopped*
- *1 celery stalk, chopped*
- *1½ cups (250g) diced red bell pepper*
- *4 cups (1l) vegetable or chicken stock*
- *4 cups (450g) roasted yellow corn kernels or drained cooked corn kernels*
- *3 cups (750ml) heavy cream*
- *2 teaspoons cumin*
- *1 teaspoon oregano*
- *1 tablespoon finely chopped cilantro*
- *salt and pepper*

**To serve:**
- **slices of country bread**
- **Vermont Cheddar cheese**
- **spoon bread**

**Patrick's update on the old South West recipe is loaded with sweet roasted yellow corn. It's gently spiced and luxuriously balanced with heavy cream. You can add shredded roast chicken and, of course, a little green chile sauce.**

**1** In a large pot on low-medium heat, melt the butter in the olive oil. Tip in the onion and stir for 5 minutes until colored. Stir in the carrot, celery, and bell pepper. Stir and cook for 5 minutes.

**2** Pour in half the stock, season lightly, bring to a simmer, and cook for 10-15 minutes, stirring a few times.

**3** Put the contents of the pot in a blender or food processor, blend, and return to the pan (you can use a hand blender).

**4** Add the corn and the rest of the stock. Simmer gently, uncovered, for 30 minutes. Stir in the cream, cumin, and herbs. Simmer for 10 minutes, or until a little reduced. Taste and adjust the seasoning.

**5** Serve piping hot, with country bread and Vermont cheddar cheese.

**St. B tip:** It may be a little time-consuming, but try roasting the red bell peppers with a sprinkling of olive oil in a hot oven for 15-20 minutes before using. Cool a little, wrap in plastic, pop in the freezer for 10 minutes and then peel off the skins. The true sweetness of the peppers will really come out.

# YELLOW CURRY ASIAN SOUP

*Serves 6-8.*

**Randy's years in Far East Asia really influenced his scented Oriental soup. He makes it very slowly over 2 days to give the flavors of the lovely broth time to brew. Don't let the cooking times put you off, it's not a difficult recipe: there's a bit of chopping and stirring involved, but the soup obligingly simmers by itself for most of the time and needs little attention.**

# RANDY'S CHICKEN STOCK

*Makes approx 3 quarts (3l).*
*Preparation and cooking 4 hours.*

- *½ **whole chicken***
- *5 **cloves garlic, crushed***
- *1 **onion, chopped***
- *3 **celery stalks, chopped***
- *2 **carrots, chopped***
- *2-3 in (5-7cm) **piece fresh ginger,** **peeled and sliced***
- *½ **teaspoon sea salt***
- *⅓ **teaspoon pepper***
- *½ **teaspoon ground cloves***
- *5 **quarts (5l) water***

**This stock is light and rich at the same time – everything a chicken stock should be – be sure to use it in other recipes.**

**1** Rinse the chicken and place it in a pot large enough to hold it comfortably with 5 quarts (5l) water and the other ingredients. Add the water, garlic, onion, celery, carrot, and ginger. Season with the salt, pepper, and cloves. Bring to a boil on medium-high heat, then reduce heat to simmer.

**2** After an hour, skim off the surface froth. Leave to simmer until the liquid is reduced by 1/3 – allow a good 3 hours.

**3** Strain the stock into another large pot. Lift out the chicken, leave to cool on a plate, cover, and refrigerate until ready to use. Discard the flavoring ingredients. Leave to get cold and refrigerate until needed (up to 3 days). You can also freeze. Skim off the surface fat before using.

# AND NOW THE ACTUAL YELLOW CURRY ASIAN SOUP...

*Preparation and cooking 2 hours.*

· **Randy's chicken stock**
**(see opposite)**
· *1 banana, peeled and chopped*
· *1 green apple, peeled and*
**chopped**
· *1 cup (240ml) coconut milk*
· *1½ tablespoons curry powder*
· *½ teaspoon ground coriander*
· *1 cup (30g) chopped*
**sourdough bread**
· *3 cloves garlic, crushed*
· *½ Vidalia onion, chopped*
· *1 medium turnip, chopped*
· *1 parsnip, chopped*
· **salt and pepper**

**To finish:**
· *1 cup (200g) diced firm tofu*
**(bite size)**
· *3 tablespoons finely chopped*
**fresh chives**

**1** Put a large pot on medium heat. Add the chicken stock, return to a simmer, and skim off the surface froth.

**2** Add the banana, apple, coconut milk, curry powder, coriander, bread, garlic, onion, turnip, and parsnip. Bring back to a simmer and cook gently for about 1 hour, until everything is very tender.

**3** While the soup is simmering, skin the chicken and remove the meat from the bones. Cut the meat into bite-size pieces. Add to the soup and return to a simmer. Keep simmering for at least 30 minutes or until ready to serve.

**4** Leave to cool a little, then blend or whiz until smooth.

**5** Just before serving, adjust the seasoning, and add the tofu and chives.

# GRASS-FED ORGANIC FILET MIGNON

*Serves 6.*
*Preparation and cooking*
*2 hours.*

· approx. *18 oz* (550g) ready-to-roast filet mignon
· *1 cup* (250g) very soft unsalted butter
· *2 teaspoons five spice powder*
· salt and pepper
· Light shallot butter sauce (see opposite)
· Pan-fried foie gras (see recipe page 132)

**Nobody compromises on quality at the St. B. Yann's filet mignon is the best you can buy. It's rightly called 'prime' for the superior flavor of the marbled meat at the core of the tenderloin. With such a great meat he chooses a simple preparation method. When you buy filet mignon to cook at home, get your butcher to clean and trim it, but ask him to keep it whole. Allow about 3 ounces (75g) per person.**

**1**  One hour before serving, rub the meat with a little soft butter. Sprinkle the five spice over one side. Put a sauté pan on very high heat. Sear the meat until browned all over. Reserve until you are ready to finish, a few minutes before serving. Keep the butter very soft in a cup or soup bowl. Keep the pan at hand (don't rinse).

**2**  Cut the meat into 6 thick slices. Dip each piece in the soft butter. Return the pan to high heat. Lightly season the meat and sizzle in the very hot pan for 4-5 seconds on each side.

**3**  Add a little Light shallot butter sauce and put a slice of Pan-fried foie gras on top of each slice. Serve immediately.

**St. B tip:** After Yann has cleaned and trimmed the meat, he places it on a cooling rack and covers it with a clean dry towel. This prevents it from coming into contact with air while it comes to room temperature.

# LIGHT SHALLOT BUTTER SAUCE

*Makes a generous cup.
Preparation and cooking
40 minutes.*

· *2 tablespoons olive oil*
· *3 shallots, finely minced*
· *1 tablespoon dried chervil*
· *1 tablespoon fresh chopped parsley*
· *⅓ cup (80ml) good red wine*
· *1 cup (240ml) good beef or vegetable stock*
· *1 cup (240ml) cold water*
· *3 tablespoons (40g) chilled butter, cut into 6 pieces*

**The shallot, herb, and wine reduction gives this sauce a good depth of flavor, and the butter gives it a soft gloss and sweet finish. Perfect with roast beef.**

**1** Put the olive oil in a heavy pan on medium heat. Add the shallots and sauté until golden. Stir in the chervil and parsley. Pour in the wine, turn up the heat a little, stir and scrape to deglaze.

**2** Reduce the heat to very low, and cook for 10 minutes to allow the alcohol in the wine to evaporate and the shallots to dissolve.

**3** Add the stock and water. Bring to a gentle boil, reduce the heat to low, and let it simmer for about 20 minutes, until the sauce is reduced by nearly half.

**4** Turn off the heat. Beat in the pieces of chilled butter one at a time. Season to taste. Keep the sauce hot sitting above a pan of simmering water (not touching the water) until needed.

# PAN-FRIED FOIE GRAS

*Serves 6.*
*Preparation and cooking*
*15 minutes.*

· *6 oz (150g) foie gras (fatted raw duck liver)*
· **salt and pepper**
· *6 thin slices fresh baguette*

**Fatted duck liver is much prized in France for its unique subtle taste of sweetly salty fat. There's no need to add butter to the pan and you'll end up with plenty of fat worth storing to use to cook eggs and meat.**

**1** With a small sharp knife, remove the veins from the liver. Cut into 6 even-sized slices. Put on a plate, cover, and refrigerate until needed.

**2** Just before serving, put a small non-stick pan on medium-high heat. Lightly season the foie gras, and fry for 4-5 minutes, until golden on both sides.

**3** Serve immediately on top of thin slices of baguette, with the filet mignon.

# FRESH PORTABELLA MUSHROOM CAPS
*with goat's cheese*

*Serves 6.*
*Marinating 1 hour, preparation and cooking 30 minutes.*

· ¾ cup (180ml) olive oil, plus extra for drizzling
· ¼ cup (60ml) balsamic vinegar
· ⅓ cup (80ml) soy sauce
· 2 tablespoons dried Mediterranean herbs or herbes de Provence
· 6 medium Portabella mushrooms, stemmed
· ⅔ cup (75g) soft goat's cheese
· 2 tablespoons heavy cream
· pepper

**Marinated meaty Portabella mushrooms have more than enough flavor to match the mild pungency and sharpness of goat's cheese. This is just as good as an appetizer as it is as a side dish–particularly if you use smaller mushrooms. If you use large mushrooms, it can be a tasty meat-free main course–satisfying enough for carnivores.**

**1** In a large bowl, mix the olive oil, balsamic vinegar, soy sauce, and 1½ tablespoons dried herbs. Whisk until frothy, add the mushrooms, and turn over until well coated. Leave to marinate for 1 hour or longer.

**2** When ready to cook, preheat the oven to 400ºF (200ºC, gas mark 6).

**3** In a bowl, mash the goat's cheese with the rest of the herbs and the cream. Season with pepper.

**4** Carefully spoon the goat's cheese filling into the mushroom caps. Drizzle with olive oil. Bake for 7-10 minutes. Serve hot.

# FRICASSÉE OF POTATOES

*with shallots and tomatoes*

*Serves 6.*
*Preparation and cooking*
*15 minutes.*

· **2 pounds (900g) Yukon potatoes,**
**skin on, scrubbed and cubed**
· **salt and pepper**
· **½ cup (125g) clarified butter**
**(see page 42)**
· **3-4 shallots, finely chopped**
· **½ cup (125g) ready-to-eat soft**
**dried tomatoes, chopped**

**There is a simple secret to crisp golden-brown potatoes and it is not to stir them while they are in the pan. Somehow it's surprisingly hard to resist the temptation to push them about while they gently sizzle. But resist you must.**

**1** Boil the potatoes in plenty of lightly salted water in a saucepan for 10-15 minutes, or until half cooked and still very firm. Drain and leave to get cold in a large bowl of iced water (add ice cubes to cold tap water). Drain again well after 5 minutes.

**2** Heat the clarified butter in a frying pan on medium high heat. Add the shallots and sauté for 3-4 minutes.

**3** Pat the potatoes dry with kitchen paper to absorb excess moisture. Add to the shallots in the pan, and stir to coat. Leave to cook without stirring for 6-8 minutes, or until the undersides of the potatoes are golden brown. Stir well to turn them over, pale sides up. Leave until the other sides are golden brown.

**4** Stir in the tomatoes, season, and serve within 5 minutes.

# DOUBLE MOUSSE AU CHOCOLAT

*Serves 12-16 people .*
*preparation 30 minutes,*
*chilling 1 hour.*

**Yann prepares a winning combination of dark and white chocolate mousses with a little crème anglaise, which few of the St. B guests can resist. You can, of course, exercise a little restraint at home and offer one mousse at a time.**

· *8* **ounces (225g) Belgian white chocolate**
· *1½* **cup (350ml) heavy cream**
· *2.5g* **leaf gelatin**
· *4* **very fresh free range eggs, separated**
· *1* **tablespoon (15g) unsalted butter**
· *2* **teaspoons Amaretto (almond liqueur)**
· *2* **teaspoons Madagascar vanilla extract (optional)**
· **Dark chocolate mousse (see recipe page 140)**

**For serving:**
· **Crème anglaise (see recipe page 141)**

**1** Cut the chocolate in small pieces. Put the pieces in the small pan of a double boiler or in a bowl that fits over a small saucepan. Put hot water in the bottom of the double boiler or in the saucepan, making sure the water does not touch the bowl. Stir occasionally with a wooden spoon until melted. Remove from the heat.

**2** Warm 1/8 cup (30ml) heavy cream to a gentle simmer in a small pan. Remove from heat, and stir in the gelatin until dissolved. Reserve in a warm place.

**3** Whisk the egg yolks until pale and frothy, reserve.

**4** Add the butter to the melted chocolate, and stir until absorbed. Add the egg yolks, stirring gently with a wooden spoon.

**5** Whisk the cream/gelatin mixture, the Amaretto, and the vanilla if using until firm. Fold into the chocolate mixture until absorbed.

**6** In a mixing bowl, beat the egg whites until soft peaks begin to form. Gently fold in the chocolate mixture.

**7** Take the soft Dark chocolate mousse out of the refrigerator. Carefully spoon the white chocolate mixture over the dark chocolate.

**8** Freeze for 40 minutes, then refrigerate for 1 hour. If you leave to set overnight, there is no need to freeze first. Serve with crème anglaise.

# DARK CHOCOLATE MOUSSE

*Serves 6 to 8.*
*Preparation 30 minutes, chilling*
*1 hour or longer.*

· *8 oz (220g) semi-unsweetened*
**Belgian dark chocolate**
· *4* **very fresh-free range eggs,**
**separated**
· *1* **tablespoon (15g) unsalted butter.**
· *1½* **cup (350ml) heavy cream.**
· *2 teaspoons Tuaca or other good*
**coffee liqueur**

**1** Cut the chocolate in small pieces with a serrated knife. Put the pieces in the small pan of a double boiler or in a bowl which fits over a small saucepan. Put water in the bottom of the double boiler or in the saucepan, making sure the water in the bottom does not touch the bowl. Stir occasionally with a wooden spoon until melted. Remove from the heat.

**2** Whisk the egg yolks until pale and frothy, reserve.

**3** Add the butter to the melted chocolate, and stir until absorbed. Add the egg yolks, stirring gently with wooden spoon. Keep in a warm place.

**4** Whisk the heavy cream and coffee liqueur until firm, fold into the chocolate mixture.

**5** In a mixing bowl, beat the egg whites until soft peaks begin to form. Gently fold in the chocolate with a spatula, working evenly from top to bottom in the same direction.

**6** Spoon into a glass bowl, and refrigerate for 1 hour if using for the Double chocolate mousse. For serving on its own, set for at least 3 hours or overnight.

# CRÈME ANGLAISE

*Serves 6 to 8.*
*Preparation and cooking 30 minutes, chilling 30 minutes.*

· *2 cups (480ml) whole milk*
· *2 teaspoons finely grated orange zest*
· *5 fresh free-range egg yolks*
· *½ cup (125g) fine baking sugar*
· *½ tablespoon cornstarch*
· *1 teaspoon vanilla pulp with seeds*

**WINE SUGGESTION:**
Ridge Geyserville, Sonoma.

**Also try this perfect light custard with poached fruit, pies and chocolate cake. Yann adds just a little cornstarch to help setting and his recipe works every time.**

**1** In a medium saucepan, bring the milk to the boil with the orange zest. While keeping an eye on the pan, in a mixing bowl, whisk the yolks, sugar and cornstarch until smooth and pale (the color of butter).

**2** Take the pan off the heat as soon as the milk starts boiling. Carefully whisk the milk into the egg yolk mixture for 2 minutes. Strain through a sieve into the saucepan.

**3** Place on medium heat, stirring constantly with a spatula, keeping the custard almost simmering until it slightly thickens, without allowing it to boil again. Test that the custard is done by drawing a line on the spatula with a finger. If the line stays clean, the custard is ready.

**4** Strain again into a fresh bowl. Add the vanilla, stir again for 3 minutes (the cream is still cooking at this stage). Let it cool at room temperature for 15 minutes. Cover the top of the custard with plastic wrap to prevent a skin forming. Leave to get cold, then refrigerate until needed.

▲

# A FEW OF THE THINGS YOU CAN DO AROUND TAOS ON AN AFTERNOON OFF THE SLOPES....

Stop at Arroyo Seco on the way, walk around, breathe in the inimitably cool sweet air, take a look at the adobe church (it may well be closed) and wander into the shops.

Immerse yourself in the arts and crafts of Northern New Mexico at the Millicent Rogers Museum. Walk through lovely traditional rooms, admiring Pueblo and Navajo jewelry, textiles, San Ildefonso pottery, Zuni and Hopi kachina dolls. Wonder at the life and talent of potter Maria Martinez. Millicent Rogers also amassed a magnificent collection of Hispanic secular and religious art. She had flawless taste and money was no object, so the museum is a gem and not to be missed. And if you can't resist museum shops, this is a good one to succumb to.

If you haven't seen it before, make a detour to see the Rio Grande Gorge. If the Taos Pueblo is open to visitors, go look at one of the oldest communities in the US. A world heritage site, it has been lived in continuously for over 1,000 years. If it's not open to visitors (and even if it is), read Frank Waters' great novel of Pueblo Indian Life, *The Man who Killed the Deer*.

Stroll around the enchanting Taos Plaza and its surroundings. Visit the galleries in Bent Street, and in Ledoux Street, shown at its Christmassy magical best on the photograph opposite by Rick Romancito, The Taos News. Ledoux Street may not may not always look as if it came straight out of a fairy tale, but it never disappoints.

Wander into La Fonda hotel for a coffee or tea. There are some extremely beautiful paintings in the handsome lobby, and some naughty pictures by D. H. Lawrence kept under lock and key. The British novelist was another victim of the magic of Taos, and his wife Frieda laid his ashes to rest in San Cristobal, some fifteen miles north of the town.

Drive on south to Ranchos de Taos, and park on the plaza near San Francisco de Asis church, look at the galleries, and admire the much painted and photographed old adobe mission church.

# WHILE IN TAOS... BUY A PAINTING

One fine day in the 60s, an artist from the Taos Pueblo, Juan Mirabal, came up to the St. Bernard. He wanted to sell his work, and of course he thought he might also be able to have a good meal at the same time. His mission was a success on both counts. Jean bought the painting and fed him handsomely. The talented painter was born in 1903 and his approach is influenced by the early Taos Moderns.

The painting had resonance for Jean at the time, and it still does. It is related to the importance of corn, the life-sustaining substance of the Pueblo people whose culture Jean admires, respects and loves.

# THURSDAY

**TALKING ABOUT THE WEATHER...**

"By now the place is really buzzing. Everyone is totally relaxed. I can't prove it scientifically, but I get the feeling the noise levels have increased. There are more conversations going on between tables. Guests are beginning to feel (not for the first time if they are regulars, but there has to be a first time for everyone) that they are part of the St. B family. Nobody talks about the end of the week. But everyone talks about the weather and the state of the snow. We have a high percentage of sunny days, that's part of Northern New Mexico's many attractions. But the sun isn't particularly good for the snow even at this high altitude. I have noticed a strange thing happening to nearly all my guests, intelligent well-educated people that they are. They all start wishing for a miracle–the constant combination of perfect fresh snow and brilliant sunshine."

▲

# MUSHROOM, HAM AND CHEESE OMELETTE

*Serves 4-6.*
*Preparation and cooking*
*30 minutes.*

· *12* **eggs**
· **salt and pepper**
· *4-5* **tablespoons (50-60g) butter**
· *½* **cup (60g) diced cooked ham**
· *1* **cup (30g) finely sliced small mushrooms**
· **cup (50g) grated Gruyère cheese**
· *1* **tablespoon finely chopped fresh herbs (parsley, tarragon, lovage, chervil or a pinch dried herbs**

**Not just an omelet, this is une omelette in the French style. The trick is to keep the eggs moist and soft.**

**1** In a bowl, whisk together the eggs with 3 tablespoons water and a pinch of salt.

**2** In a small frying pan, melt a little butter over a medium heat and sauté the ham in it until a little colored. Tip onto a plate and reserve. Add a little more butter to the pan, sauté the mushrooms for 3-5 minutes, season lightly and reserve with the ham.

**4** Put a non-stick sauté pan over a medium high heat. Add 2 tablespoons (25g) butter. As soon as the foaming subsides, pour in the eggs, swirl until almost set. Scatter the cheese down the center of the omelet(te) mixture, spread the ham and mushroom on top. Using a spatula and tilting the pan, fold 1/3 omelet(te) over the filling on one side, then fold over 1/3 omelet(te) from the opposite side. The filling should be entirely covered and the omelet(te) should look like a long fat envelope.

**4** Using a spatula or fish slice, carefully turn the omelet(te) over and cook for 30 seconds. Slide onto a warm plate. Brush with butter and sprinkle with herbs. Serve immediately.

# SANTA FE OMELETTE

Follow the same method, omit the ham, mushrooms and Gruyère cheese filling. Replace with 1 cup (40g) sautéed chopped chorizo, and ½ cup (120ml) fresh salsa made with 1 diced tomato, 3 tablespoons finely chopped cilantro, 1 finely chopped scallion and the juice from 1 wedge of lime. If you like, also add to the filling ½ cup (50g) grated mild Cheddar. Garnish with 1 finely diced small ripe avocado. Chris fills a classic French omelette with the tastes of New Mexico.

▲

# CARROT SOUP

*Serves 4-6.*
*Preparation and cooking*
 *1½ hours.*

· *3 shallots, finely diced*
· *4 cups (400g) diced carrots*
· *2 scallions, minced*
· *1½ quarts (1½ l) white*
**vegetable stock (see page 19)**
· *1 cup (240ml) heavy cream*
· **pepper**

**This subtly flavored carrot soup is extremely smooth and soothing. Try the same method for making cauliflower or broccoli soup.**

**1** In a heavy pan, melt the butter over medium heat. Add the shallots, sauté for 3 minutes, then add the carrots and scallions. Sauté for 3-5 minutes. .

**2** Pour over the stock, bring to a boil, reduce the heat, add the cream, and simmer gently for at least 1 hour.

**3** If you like, blend or whiz before serving. Season with a little pepper and serve very hot.

# STEVE'S SAUERKRAUT

*Serves 4-6.*
*Preparation and cooking*
*1¼ hours.*

· *1 tablespoon (15g) butter or oil*
· *½ pound (225g) bacon, chopped*
· *2 cups (480 ml) dark beer, such*
**as Negro Meldo**
· *3 cups (1kg) rinsed sauerkraut*
· *3 tablespoons juniper berries*
· *2 tablespoons caraway seed*

**Juniper berries, beer, and caraway seed turn sauerkraut into a class act. Serve with sausages, chicken, duck, or pork tenderloin. The sauerkraut will keep for 2-3 days covered and refrigerated.**

**1** Put the butter or oil a heavy braising or frying pan or over a medium high heat. Add the bacon, and cook until it colors and releases its fat. Pour in the beer, turn up the heat a little and bring to a boil, stirring.

**2** Add the sauerkraut, juniper berries, and caraway seed. Reduce the heat to low and simmer gently for 1 hour, stirring occasionally.

# BAVARIANS BEWARE: JEAN HAS A WAY WITH APFEL STRUDEL

Being Parisian, I have to admit I have a hard time doing a real apfel strudel. However, we do make a version that people seem to like—maybe it's because we serve it *mit Schlag*! Take 4 apples, juicy but not too sweet. Cut them into small pieces, sprinkle over a little lemon juice to bring out the apple juice and add a little tartness.

On a flat surface, place the dough. You could use Brisée pastry dough (page 81) but let's use a phyllo dough! The reason for doing this is that most people (I mean myself) sometimes have difficulty doing pastry dough the right way. It's too thick, too thin, and not pliable enough... Irritating. With phyllo dough you can buy it and use it as is.

Carefully place the apples on 2-3 sheets of phyllo. You can also sprinkle with a small handful of raisins. Roll the dough around the apples Keep it round or make it into a square. Sprinkle over 1 or 2 tablespoons brown sugar. Lightly beat 1 egg yolk with 2 teaspoons water. Paint this over the rolled dough to help it caramelize. Put on a baking tray, bake in an oven preheated to 375°F (190°C, gas mark 5) for about 20 minutes until the apples are tender and the phyllo is golden brown.

You can sprinkle the apples with a tablespoon of Calvados or apple brandy before cooking. And to make it look Bavarian... you must serve the strudel in thick 3in (7.5cm) slices, with whipped cream (here comes the Schlag!). Remember to add a little yodeling as you serve!

# WATERCRESS BROTH

*Serves 6-8.*
*Preparation and cooking 1 hour.*

**Tangy peppery watercress grown in water comes to a perfect full circle in this pale golden clear soup. If all comfort food could be this light and healthy... If you like, add shredded chicken from the stock.**

**For the watercress broth:**
· **¼ cup (50g) clarified butter**
· **¼ cup (60ml) olive oil**
· **1 small onion, finely chopped**
· **3 cloves garlic, finely chopped**
· **1 cup (175g) yellow squash cut to bite size**
· **⅓ cup (80ml) dry sherry**
· **2 quarts (2l) Randy's chicken stock (see St. B tip below)**
· **leaves picked from ½ pound (225g) fresh watercress**

**For the garnish:**
· **3-4 whole garlic cloves**
· **olive oil to cover**

**1** Heat the butter and olive oil on medium heat in a small pan. Toss in the onion and garlic, and sauté for 2-3 minutes.

**2** Add the squash, and sauté 1-2 minutes. Turn up the heat a little, add the sherry and cook, stir for 2 minutes to deglaze. Remove from the heat.

**3** Put with the strained chicken stock in a large pot. Heat until simmering over a medium heat.

**4** For the garnish, put the whole garlic cloves in the small pan, cover with olive oil, and cook over medium heat for ½ hour or until the cloves are golden brown. Take off the heat and strain over a bowl – save the garlic-flavored oil for future use. Chop the roasted garlic finely and set aside.

**5** Add the watercress leaves to the simmering stock, and continue simmering for 5 minutes. Adjust the seasoning.

**6** Serve hot garnished with the chopped roasted garlic.

**St. B tip:** Make the Chicken stock as instructed on page 124, leaving out the cloves and ginger. Add ½ cup each diced turnip and parsnip, 2 bay leaves, and a teaspoon each dried dill and tarragon.

# CANARD À L'ORANGE

*Serves 4.*
*Preparation and cooking*
*3½ hours.*

· *5 pounds (2.3kilo) ready-for-roasting duck at room temperature*
· **salt and pepper**
· **a few pieces orange peel**
· **a few sprigs fresh or dry thyme**
· *2* **bay leaves**
· *1* **small onion, chopped**
· *1* **carrot, chopped**
· *1* **celery stalk, chopped**
· *1* **tablespoon olive oil**

**For serving:**
· **Orange sauce with Grand Marnier (see page 159)**

**The St. B's duck with orange is joyfully traditional. It comes with orange baskets made by cutting the peel of whole oranges in the shape of baskets with a handle, then carefully scooping out the flesh. Each table gets a basket filled with sauce, with Jean making a great show of pouring the sauce over the duck. The secret is to use good-quality duck (the St. B likes Long Island ducks) and to roast them first at a very high heat, then very low and slow for over 2 hours. To add to the excitement of the occasion, one of the chefs even once let loose a live duck in the dining room as Jean was serving the duck.**

**1** Preheat the oven to 450ºF (230ºC, gas mark 8). Season the duck all over. Put the orange peel and dry thyme inside the cavity. Put the bay leaves, onion, carrot, and celery in the center of a roasting pan. Sprinkle over the olive oil. Place the duck on top. Roast for 20 minutes.

**2** Take out of the oven, turn the duck over, return to the oven. Reduce the heat to 300ºF (150ºC, gas mark 2) and roast for 30 minutes more. Turn the duck on one side and remove some of the fat from the pan. Continue roasting the duck for 2 hours, turning 2 or 3 times and removing some of the fat as you do.

**3** Once the duck is very tender and the juices come out pale yellow-brown, pour the juices into a bowl. Put in the freezer for 10 minutes. Let the duck stand in the turned-off oven for at least 15 minutes before serving.

**4** Just before serving, take out the bowl with the duck juices. Skim off the fat from the surface, and add the juices to the orange sauce.

**5** Carve the duck and serve hot with the orange sauce.

# ORANGE SAUCE

*with Grand Marnier*

*Makes ¼ cups.*
*Preparation and cooking*
*40 minutes.*

· **2 tablespoons (25g) butter**
**at room temperature and**
**2 tablespoons (25g) chilled butter,**
**cut into 4 pieces**
· **2 shallots, finely diced**
· **2 teaspoons paprika**
· **small pinch pepper**
· **⅓ cup (80ml) good red wine**
· **3 tablespoons balsamic vinegar**
· **1 tablespoon sugar**
· **2 tablespoons Grand Marnier**
**or Cointreau**
· **1 cup (240ml) orange juice**
· **3 pieces orange peel**
· **½ cup (120ml) chicken or**
**vegetable stock**

**1** Put the butter in a heavy pan over a medium heat. Add the shallots, and sauté until golden.

**2** Stir in the paprika, pepper, wine, vinegar, sugar, Grand Marnier, orange juice and peel. Turn up the heat a little, and stir until bubbling. Reduce the heat to low, and cook for 10 minutes.

**3** Add the stock and ½ cup (120ml) water. Bring to a gentle boil, reduce the heat to low, and let it simmer for about 20 minutes until the sauce is reduced by nearly half. Turn off the heat.

**4** Beat in the pieces of chilled butter one at a time. Taste and adjust the seasoning. Keep the sauce hot sitting above a pan of simmering water (not touching the water) until needed.

**To serve, shrimps créole:** Jean serves juicy large Louisiana shrimp at the same time as the duck: ' ... the contrast is very successful. We clean the tail-on shrimp in salted water and sauté them quickly in hot olive oil seasoned with diced tomato and red bell pepper, cayenne and a touch of Tabasco. We then simmer them briefly over hot rock salt for extra flavor. They end up being so succulent that people want to eat them with their fingers.'

# SWEET POTATO GRATIN

*Serves 6-8.*
*Preparation and cooking*
*1½ hours.*

· *2-2½* pounds (1.25kg) sweet potatoes, scrubbed, skin on
· ½ cup (50g) finely grated high quality Parmesan cheese
· ½ cup (125g) clarified butter (see page 42)
· *1 teaspoon salt*
· ½ teaspoon white pepper

**Randy's golden gratin is crispy on the outside and tender inside. It's easy to make, with the exception of the flipping over. The Art of the Flipping Over looks deceptively easy when a pro does it, but it can be quite a challenge if you haven't had years of practice. A solution is to cover the pan with a slightly larger plate. Using oven mitts and holding plate and pan tightly together, turn the whole thing over so that the potatoes sit on the plate golden side down. Carefully slip back into the pan.** *Voilà!*

**1** Put the potatoes in a large pot, pour in water to cover completely. Bring water to a boil, reduce to a simmer, and cook the potatoes 35-40 minutes until 80% done. The potatoes should still feel a little firm when you test the flesh with a metal skewer or point of a knife.

**2** Strain at once. Immediately tip potatoes into a large bowl filled with water and ice cubes to cool them quickly from the core out. Strain and leave to dry. After drying, the skin should be easy to remove by hand, but you might require a peeler in some spots.

**3** Using a cheese grater, grate the potatoes into a bowl. Add the Parmesan cheese and season with the salt and pepper. Mix thoroughly.

**4** Put a large sauté pan over a medium-high heat, add the clarified butter, and heat to almost but not quite burning point. Tip in the potato mixture, lightly press out towards the sides to fill the pan and smooth down the surface. After 4-5 minutes, slightly lift the potatoes to check that they have turned a dark golden brown. Carefully flip over to cook the other side in the same way. Don't worry about little brown spots caused by the sugar in the potatoes caramelizing.

**5** Slip into a dish and serve hot.

# WARM ARTICHOKE HEARTS

*with smoked trout, capers, aniseed & feta*

*Serves 6.*
*Preparation and cooking 1 hour,*
*marinating 1 hour.*

· *1 tablespoon (15g) unsalted butter*
· *1 large red onion, thinly sliced*
· *2 teaspoons capers*
· *½ tablespoon whole anise seeds*
· *½ cup (120ml) vinegar*
· *2 tablespoon red wine*
· *2 tablespoonsp honey*
· *½ tablespoon dry tarragon*
· *¼ cup (60ml) fruity olive oil*
· *1 teaspoon ground coriander*
· *1 tablespoon lemon juice*
· *1½ tablespoons white wine*
· *6 uncooked whole artichoke hearts*
· *6 pieces smoked trout*
· *2 tablespoons crumbled*
*feta cheese*
· *salt and pepper*

**Yann uses whole artichoke hearts frozen raw—no need to defrost first. If you can only find cooked artichoke hearts or bottoms, marinate as described, and steam for just 10 minutes until hot. This lovely dish has a subtle mix of flavors. Serve St. B-style alongside the main course, but also try as a starter. Your guests will be impressed either way.**

**1** Melt the butter in a frying pan on medium heat. Sauté the red onion for 5 minutes, or until golden brown.

**2** Add 1 ½ tablespoons cold water. Reduce the heat, add the capers and anise seeds, and sauté for 15 minutes until caramelized. Cover and set aside.

**3** At the same time, in a small saucepan, bring the vinegar and red wine to a gentle boil. Stir in the honey and tarragon, and return to a boil. Reduce the heat, let it cook gently for 15 minutes until reduced and thick. Reserve to use as a dressing.

**4** In a bowl, whisk together the olive oil, coriander, lemon juice, and white wine. Add the artichoke hearts. Stir to coat them in the mixture and leave to marinate 1 hour.

**5** At the end of that time, lift the artichoke hearts out of the marinade. Put them in a steaming basket or tray, pour the marinade in a pan, and top up with water. Put the basket or tray on top of the pan, cover tightly, and steam for about 40 minutes, until just tender.

**6** Put the artichokes on 6 small plates (or in small dishes or ramekins), add a good spoonful of the caramelized onions and caper mixture. Set a piece of smoked trout on top, add a little crumbled feta cheese. Spoon over the warm dressing, season with pepper, and, if you like, keep in a just warm oven for 10 minutes before serving.

# CRÈME BRÛLÉE

*Makes 8 small ramekins. Preparation, infusing and cooking 1½ hours, cooling and refrigerating at least 1½ hours, caramelizing, 5-10 minutes.*

· *1 fresh mango, peeled, stone removed and flesh diced*
· *2 cups (475ml) heavy cream*
· *¼ cup (50g) fine sugar*
· *1½ teaspoons finely grated orange zest*
· *3 pieces dried star anise*
· *4 free-range egg yolks*
· *2 teaspoons Madagascar vanilla extract*
· *2 tablespoons each Turbinado sugar and fine white sugar for the caramel*
· *8 fresh raspberries, to decorate*

**WINE SUGGESTION:**
Domaine Drouhin.

**A word of warning from Yann: this is very rich custard, so use very small ramekins. If you can, make the day before to give the delicate flavors of the 'burnt cream' time to develop.**

**1** Put the ramekins 1 inch (2.5cm) apart in a deep ovenproof pan. Divide the diced mango between the ramekins, and set aside. In a small saucepan, bring to a gentle boil the cream and the sugar on medium heat. Add the orange zest and star anise. Take the pan off heat, and let the cream infuse for 30 minutes.

**2** In a bowl, beat by hand the yolks until pale. Bring a full kettle of water to the boil. Preheat the oven to 275ºF (140ºC, gas mark 1).

**3** Return the pan to the heat and bring the cream back to a gentle boil. Pour two-thirds of the cream over the yolks, mix well, then pour the mixture back into the saucepan. Mix well, take off the heat, and strain through a fine sieve into a bowl. Stir in the vanilla, and leave to cool for 5 minutes.

**4** Pour the mixture into the ramekins, filling them almost to the top. Pour boiling water into the pan to come halfway up ramekins. Bake for 20 minutes, carefully rotate each ramekin by 180º, and bake for a further 25 minutes.

**5** Take the pan out of the oven, lift out the ramekins and leave to cool to room temperature. Once cool, refrigerate for at least 1 hour, longer if possible. Cover the ramekins with plastic wrap if leaving overnight.

**6** Shortly before serving, caramelize the custard: mix all the sugars, sprinkle over the ramekins (not too thickly). Using a cooking torch (or a plumber's torch, taking care not to burn yourself and the ramekins), caramelize the sugar until it becomes like a thin layer of brown 'glass' – don't let it get black. If you don't have a torch, try broiling close to the top of the oven at a very high heat for 2- 3 minutes, until crisp and golden brown. Leave to rest for 2 minutes. Add a raspberry to each ramekin, and serve.

# MATCHING WINE AND FOOD—AND THE BAR AT THE ST. BERNARD

This won't come as a surprise to regulars of the hotel but the St. B's wine list really reflects the quality of the cooking. It will do justice to the menu, whether you hesitate between a Pouilly Fumé and a Sancerre to accompany the salmon or paella for your table, or just want a glass of house Sauvignon Blanc or Chardonnay. Evan Blish is the man in charge of the wine cellar. In keeping with the St.B's unique brand of Franco-American entente cordiale, his selection for la cave combines classics from both the Old and the New World, with personal discoveries he enjoyed on trips to vineyards or in tastings with serious connoisseurs from Berkeley, who come up every year to sample and discuss wines with him. Evan is a serious wine buff but he wears his knowledge lightly. At the St. B every evening around 6pm, there is a happy run-up to dinner when everyone congregates near the bar and in the dining room around the glowing fireplace, or tries to decipher Jean's handwritten menu on the board above the service counter. This is the time when many guests select a wine for their meal. Evan and Jean are around to make suggestions that will suit the diners. You can be guided to a Super Tuscan, a Gigondas or a Domaine Drouhin from Oregon without fuss or over-elaborate descriptions. After decades of observation, Evan can tell you a thing or two about people from their choice of wines. He has observed that people from New York tend to prefer French wines while Californians stick to the fruit of their local vineyards. Before the season starts, he talks to the chefs about dishes to help make his selection. The trend is for a greater choice of interesting wines by the glass.

New Mexico has a growing wine business. The most popular domestic local brand at the St.B is the sparkling Blanc de Noir Gruet, dry, light and a perfect informal fizz. It's a perfect pre-dinner drink, if you don't succumb to the delicious house Margarita mixed by Evan or by Michael Kierst—another man who came for a season and is still there every winter a few decades later, enjoying the snow when not pulling one of the five beers on tap and chatting with the habitués.

# FRIDAY

## FRIDAY CAME TOO FAST

"Today is the last day of the ski-week and people feel a little sad to leave, a little nostalgic in advance–somehow they begin to miss the place before they leave it. This is the time when friends make plans to come back at the same time next season. Instructors are invited to eat lunch or have a drink to acknowledge the fun and camaraderie of the week. The send-off dinner is quite spectacular. The chefs excel themselves at preparing a great feast of a meal, a menu that has become a St. B tradition. There's a little soup, then a fragrant smooth fondue. After the food of the Alps comes the best of the Wild West, a prime rib of buffalo, served with a gratin of lentil and zucchini. And to round off the extravaganza, I bring in crêpe suzette and show off my skills at flambéing. If the mood is right, I might be persuaded to sing a little–most guests can sing along with 'alouette' or hum 'la vie en rose'. I tend to slip out quietly afterwards while the end-of-term party goes on."

# POACHED EGGS

*with smoked salmon, cream cheese, tomatoes & capers*

*Serves 4.*
*Preparation and cooking*
*30 minutes.*

· *4* **mini bagels or** *2* **bagels, split into halves**
· *1* **tablespoon (15g) soft butter**
· **¼ cup (60ml) white vinegar**
· *4* **eggs**
· *6-8* **tablespoons cream cheese**
· *1* **tablespoon capers, drained if brined**
· *1* **tablespoon finely chopped red onion**
· *4* **small slices lox**
· *1½* **tablespoons diced tomato**
· *1* **tablespoon finely chopped fresh parsley**

**1** Toast the bagels, and butter lightly while still hot. If you prefer, fry the bagels with butter in a frying pan. Set aside.

**2** In a saucepan or deep sauté pan, heat 4 inches (10cm) water and the vinegar until simmering. Maintaining the simmer, carefully break 2 eggs into the liquid and poach. As soon as the egg whites have set around the yolks, lift out from the pan with a slotted spoon. Place on a dish lined with kitchen paper to drain. Poach the 2 remaining eggs in the same way.

**3** Spread the cream cheese on the bagels. Scatter over the capers and red onion, add the lox and diced tomato. Put an egg on top, sprinkle with parsley and serve as soon as possible.

# TUNA SALADE NIÇOISE ST. BERNARD

Originally a simple raw dish of tomato and lettuce with anchovies, Salade Niçoise has become a great light meal popular all over the world. Jean, who lived and studied in Nice, is an expert at the beautiful salad: "True enough there were no potatoes or cooked vegetables in the original, but I lived in Nice and this is the way we liked-and still like-our salade niçoise. Take a big clear glass bowl to be able to enjoy the colors, put in butter lettuce and a little frisée (not too much, it's a bit of a mouthful). Now place above the leaves some cooked French beans, diced boiled new potatoes, thinly sliced red or sweet white onion, chopped basil, a little thyme, sliced ripe tomatoes, half a boiled egg per person and shreds of canned tuna. Yes, canned-not seared fresh tuna-it tastes much better in this salad and that is the way we do it in Nice. Put anchovies on the egg. You can also add slivers of green bell peppers. All you now need is to douse the salad with Balsamic garlic vinaigrette. And, I almost forgot, lovely small Nice olives."

# BALSAMIC GARLIC VINAIGRETTE

*Makes 3-4 cups.*
*Preparation 15 minutes.*

· *1 teaspoon Dijon mustard*
· **salt and pepper**
· *3-4 tablespoons balsamic vinegar*
· *2-3 cloves garlic, crushed*
· **2 shallots, very finely chopped**
· **yolk of** *1* **very fresh free-range egg**
· **½ cup (120ml) fruity olive oil**
· *1-2 teaspoons lemon juice*
· **1 tablespoon finely chopped fresh parsley**

**You shouldn't taste the oil in the vinaigrette, if you use enough vinegar and salt. The trick is to taste and experiment until you are happy with the flavors...**

**1** In a bowl, mix the mustard with a little salt and pepper, the vinegar, garlic, and shallots. Bind with the egg yolk.

**2** Still beating vigorously, work in the olive oil until the mixture emulsifies. Taste and adjust the seasoning (add just enough salt so that you can no longer taste any oiliness). Add the lemon juice and parsley at the end.

**3** Cover the leftover garlic vinaigrette and refrigerate until you next need it. Use within 48 hours.

# FRENCH LEEK AND POTATO SOUP

*Serves 4-6.*
*Preparation and cooking*
*1¾ hours.*

· 4 tablespoons (50g) butter
· 3-4 medium leeks, thinly sliced
· 4-6 medium russet potatoes,
diced and reserved in cold water
· salt and pepper
· ½-1 cup (120-240ml) heavy or
light cream
· ½ cup (20g) finely chopped chives

In good cooking (Jean would tell you the same applies to skiing and many other things in life), the secret is in the detail... Even for a simple dish like this leek and potato soup, Chris recommends you take great care when you adjust the seasoning: 'I have noticed it can take a lot more salt than you'd expect. There aren't many ingredients, so salt is an important element of the flavor.' You can make the soup thicker or thinner by changing the ratio of potato to water. A thinner soup might be good in the summer, a thicker one more suitable in the winter. The same goes for the cream: adjust to make more or less rich in taste and feeling. Chris prepares the soup French country style-half blended, with small neat pieces of vegetables. You can make it more rustic and skip the blending. If you prefer to whiz the soup completely into an elegant creamy little number, save preparation time by simply roughly chopping the leeks and potatoes.

**1** Put a 6-8 quart (6-8l) stockpot over a medium heat, then add the butter. When the bubbling subsides, stir in the leeks. Stir and cook until a little golden in color.

**2** Drain the potatoes and add to the pot. Stir and add enough water to cover potatoes and leeks completely with extra 1-2 in (3-5cm) water on top. Add 3 tablespoons salt, simmer for 1 hour, or until the potatoes are tender.

**3** Ladle ¼-½ of the soup into a blender and blend until smooth. Return to the pot. Add the cream, taste, and adjust the seasoning with extra salt and with pepper. Return to a simmer. Finish off with a sprinkling of chives.

# ALPINE FONDUE

*with Prosciutto & French country bread*

*Serves 6.*
*Preparation and cooking*
*35-40 minutes.*

· ½ **pound (250g) Swiss**
**Alpenzeller cheese**
· *6 ounces (200g)* **Gruyère cheese**
· *6 ounces (200g)* **Emmental cheese**
· *1 cup (240ml)* **Kirsch**
· *3 cups (700ml)* **white wine**
· *2 bay leaves*
· *2 teaspoons freshly*
**grated nutmeg**
· **pepper**

**To serve:**
· ½ **French baguette, cut into**
**neat cubes**
· *6 slices of Italian Prosciutto*
· *12 cornichons*
**(small French gherkins)**

**As a rule, allow about 3 ounces (90g) cheese per person. The cheese mixture will start getting firmer the moment you take the pot off the heat so, if you have a fondue set somewhere, this is the moment to give it an airing - take it out and use it. Your fondue will stay nicer longer.**

**1** Shred all the cheeses for easier melting. In a small pan, bring the kirsch to a simmer. Remove from the heat, and carefully set alight with a long match. Leave the flames to die down, cover, and reserve.

**2** In a fondue pot or a heavy pan, bring to a simmer 1½ cups (350ml) wine with the bay leaves. Cover the fondue pot, reduce the heat, and simmer gently for 10 minutes until well infused. Put the rest of the wine in a separate pan and heat until barely simmering.

**3** Lift out the bay leaves, and bring heat to high. Pour in all the cheese at once, and start stirring with a wooden spoon in a figure-of-eight. Reduce heat to low. The stirring must be done in the same direction, and at a constant speed. Add the rest of the white wine, and stir continuously until all the wine is absorbed and the cheese has melted to a smooth uniform aspect. Season with the nutmeg and a little pepper.

**4** Reheat the Kirsch until almost simmering, then pour it into the pot. Stir until the fondue is smooth and a little liquid.

**5** Serve immediately, with small chunks of French bread. Put on the table a plate of prosciutto and small French gherkins.

# PRIME RIB OF BUFFALO

*with wild mushrooms, sweet vermouth & raisins*

*Serves 6.*
*Preparation and cooking 7 hours.*

· **½ buffalo prime rib (4 bone rib)**
· **salt and pepper**
· **1 cup (240ml) grapeseed oil**
· **¾ cup (175g) clarified butter**
· **1 large Vidalia onion, chopped**
· **3 stalks celery, chopped**
· **4 carrots, peeled and chopped**
· **8-10 cloves garlic, chopped**
· **1 cup (240ml) red wine**
· **12 floz (400ml) can beer**
· **⅓ cup (80ml) tomato paste**
· **2 tablespoons Dijon mustard**
· **3 tablespoons chopped fresh parsley leaves**
· **1 tablespoon chopped fresh tarragon leaves**
· **1 tablespoon fresh thyme leaves**
· **¼ cup (60ml) rice wine vinegar**
· **3 cups (700ml) beef or chicken stock**
· **1½ cups (75g) chopped wild mushrooms (chanterelles, shitake, trumpets)**
· **¼ cup (60ml) sweet vermouth or port**
· **1 cup (150g) golden raisins**

**A stunning party piece for very special occasions. Start bringing the rib to room temperature in the morning, put the meat in the oven at lunch time and leave to roast very gently while you get on with your day.**

**1** Leave the rib roast to sit at room temperature for 3 hours. Coat the meat at the top with salt and pepper. Preheat the oven to 200-210°F, 100°C mark 1/4. Heat a very large heavy frying pan or flat pancake pan to medium-high, add oil to the hot surface. Sear the rib roast, top meat facing down, over high heat. Carefully holding the top end, rock the rib to sear as much of the meat as you can. Remove from the heat once it is uniformly colored.

**2** Heat a sauté pan over a medium high heat, add ½ cup (120g) clarified butter, the onion, celery, carrots, and garlic, and sauté for 3-4 minutes. Pour in the wine, and stir well until bubbling. Remove from the heat, add the beer, tomato paste, Dijon mustard, parsley, tarragon, thyme, and vinegar. Stir well. Pour the sautéed mixture into an oven roasting pan large enough to hold the rib. Place the rib on top. Cover the roasting pan.

**3** Roast the rib in the oven for 5-6 hours. After 5 hours, check for doneness with a meat thermometer, the internal temperature should read at 140-145°F (60-65°C) for rare to medium-rare. Take out of oven, turn off heat, and close door. Remove rib from pan and put on a dish. Place the roasting pan with the flavoring ingredients over a medium heat. Add the stock, stir, simmer for ½ hour.

**4** Put the rest of the butter in a sauté pan over medium heat, and sauté the mushrooms for 3-4 minutes. Add the vermouth, cook for 2-3 minutes. Remove from the heat. Strain the contents of the roasting pan into a saucepan, add the mushrooms and raisins. Adjust seasoning. Keep over a low heat for 30 minutes.

**5** Put the rib back in the roasting pan, cover, return to the warm turned-off oven until ready to serve. Serve with the mushroom and raisin sauce.

# GRATIN OF LENTILS

*with yellow zucchini*

*Serves 6.*
*Preparation and cooking 7 hours.*

- *2 cups (400g) small puy lentils*
- *2 bay leaves*
- **salt and pepper**
- *1 stick (125g) butter*
- *2-3 shallots, finely chopped*
- *3-4 cloves garlic, minced*
- *2 zucchini, cut into bite size chunks*
- **2 small Roma tomatoes, chopped**
- **½ tablespoon dried Mediterranean herbs or Herbes de Provence**

**This colorful dish makes a good accompaniment to roast chicken, pork, and lamb, as well as buffalo rib. It is also a nice well-balanced vegetarian main course. Stir in a little freshly grated cheese for extra protein when you combine the lentils and vegetables.**

**1** Put the lentils in a pot and cover with cold water coming up 1 inch (2.5cm) above the lentils. Add the bay leaves and season with salt and pepper. Bring to a boil, reduce the heat, and cover. Simmer until tender, anything from 25 minutes to 1 hour depending on the lentils. Check after 25 minutes, you don't want the lentils to become mushy. Remove from the heat, strain, refresh with cold water, strain again, and set aside.

**2** Melt the butter in a sauté pan over a medium high heat, sauté the shallots and garlic for 3-4 minutes. Add the zucchini, tomatoes, and herbs, and cook for a further 5 minutes. Season to taste.

**3** Gently combine the lentils with the sautéed vegetables before serving. If you like, you can prepare ahead: put in an oven pan, cover, and keep in a warm oven until ready to serve.

# FLAMING CRÊPES SUZETTE

*with Grand Marnier*

*Serves 6 (makes 12 small crêpes or a giant crêpe). Preparation and cooking 45 minutes.*

- ¼ cup (60ml) milk
- 3 egg yolks
- 1 tablespoon granulated sugar
- 1 cup (240ml) Cointreau or Grand Marnier
- ½ cup (75g) sifted all purpose flour
- 5 tablespoons (80g) melted or clarified butter, plus extra for greasing the pan

Orange sauce:
- 1 orange, peeled, inner skin removed, finely chopped
- 3 tablespoons (45g) unsalted butter
- 1½ cups (350ml) fresh orange juice fine sugar to taste
- 3 tablespoons crème fraîche or heavy cream

For flaming:
- Cognac

**WINE SUGGESTION:**
Cabernet Sauvignon, Napa.

Chris started a new trend at the St. B when he cooked a large pancake for each table instead of the more usual individual crêpes. After Jean has made his customary great oh-la-la show of pouring the flaming sauce over the crêpe for his appreciative audience, the person serving his or her table divides it between the guests. It's quicker to serve, which means everyone can enjoy their crêpe piping-hot.

1 Prepare the sauce: put the orange flesh, butter, orange juice, and Cointreau or Grand Marnier in a small saucepan over medium-high heat, and add sugar to taste. Stir until bubbling, then cook for 5 minutes and stir in the crème fraîche or cream. Keep on a low heat until required.

2 Make the batter: blend the yolks, granulated sugar, Cointreau or Grand Marnier, sifted flour, and melted butter at top speed for 1 minute. Leave the batter to rest for at lest 15 minutes.

3 Grease a pancake pan. Heat over a high-medium heat until very hot. Test the heat and batter by spooning out a tablespoon of batter onto the pan. Cook for a minute until the underside is light brown, flip over with a spatula, and cook the other side for 30-40 seconds.

4 To make each pancake, ladle just enough batter to cover the pan, then cook as above. Fold or roll and keep as warm as possible.

5 To serve, heat the cognac in a small pan. Carefully pour into the sauce, set alight with a taper or very long match, then pour the flaming sauce over the folded or rolled pancakes.

**St.B tip:** Try filling the pancakes with a little fruit compote: melt 1/2 stick (30g) butter, stir in a handful of berries, 2 tablespoons brown sugar, a handful of raisins. and a chopped peeled orange. Simmer for 30 minutes.

# SUMMERTIME RIO GRANDE

The joys of summer: paddling upright on the Rio Grande. When there's no snow left to ski, Jean windsurfs surfs in Hawaii during his vacation or paddles on the Rio Grande. The great river is at its most magnificent twenty-odd miles down from the Ski Valley. Each summer, music students are treated to an unforgettable picnic in a spectacular spot overlooking the river on the western side of the John Dunn Bridge. You get to your destination after a bumpy drive on dusty dirt roads. The blue of the sky deepens and turns magical as the evening approaches. If you are lucky, you'll see a curtain of rain moving along in the distance, in a corner of the vast horizon. Jean will tell you that it is known as 'walking rain'.

# SUMMERTIME AND THE SCHOOL OF MUSIC

It is early July in Taos Ski Valley. The mountains are green and redolent with wildflowers. There are horses for hire at the top of Strawberry Hill. The ski village is quiet and dozy as if in the middle of a very long siesta, but violin and cello music is pouring out of the open windows of the St. Bernard. The sound is live, stopping and starting, punctuated by comments and laughter. Winter guests may well think the St. B they know and love goes into some sort of hibernation under dust covers at the end of the ski season, with occasional bursts of activity for repairs and maintenance. They are partly right, but every June since 1963 the hotel welcomes the annual Taos School of Music. For eight weeks it becomes home to a group of nineteen carefully auditioned young musicians. They are fresh-faced, talented, and eager to play, working assiduously with three leading chamber orchestras that take turns to help them prepare four major concerts down in the Taos Community Auditorium as well as at the St. B.

A stage and a large piano are set up in the dining room. Come breakfast-time, Jean is at his station behind the counter, dishing out Santa Fe omelets with a smile, and perhaps a sparkle of amused tolerance: you couldn't really describe the music students as early birds. There's no brisk morning buzz and anticipation of a day on the slopes. Around 8 am the dining room is quiet and empty; yawning young people trickle in a few at a time. Breakfast is leisurely, nobody appears to be in a hurry to start working early in the morning—but discussions and practice have gone on late into the night. The students' laid-back attitude is deceptive: they are here to improve their skills and technique. It is an ideal opportunity to talk, live, and breathe music in a relaxed atmosphere, and the best of locations with like-minded fellow musicians.

...

The days are warm and dry, the sky clear and blue, the air thin as ever, high clouds building up into a mini monsoon early most afternoons, temperatures dropping sharply at night. Mornings are cool and as fresh as if the earth were new. You can walk up the Rubezahl trail between the pines, towering six feet higher in summer than they do above the snow's thick mattress. Across the trees you glimpse an ice-free (somehow it's a surprise) Beaver Creek. If you are too lazy to hike down the grassy slopes from the top of Chair 1, you are faced with a vertiginous ride down, clutching the narrow bar that separates you from the void. It's not an experience for the faint of heart: even Jean has been heard to confide that he didn't enjoy the—for him—unusual experience of being stuck there not able to control the situation and ski his way out. Ski week regulars who happen to be visiting might just feel they've landed in a parallel universe...

▲

# MARIE-PIERRE'S EPILOGUE

I am writing these lines by the sea in Paramé, Brittany. It's one of my favorite places, solid unostentatious houses keeping watch on a long sand beach that disappears at high tide, kite surfers defying gravity, fast moving clouds, grand peaceful sunsets, the roar of the sea that's always the same and always different. I have just received an email from Jean mentioning that Paramé close to the ramparts of Saint Malo was the birthplace of his mother. I think of the distant St. B, look up at the sky (not as high and vast and intense as in New Mexico but pretty good for little old Europe) and picture the ski valley thousands of miles away to the west in another continent and twelve thousand feet (OK, 3 kilometres in local measurements) above where I am sitting. Memories flood back, voices telling me stories in many accents, laughter in the kitchen, learning to flounce table napkins in the approved St. B manner, young musicians rehearsing while I work in my little corner of the dining room looking at wild flowers and green mountains. The scene shifts to winter, to the buzz of breakfast, then the sudden quiet that descends on the hotel once the door has closed on the last tardy skier running late, to the exhilarating feeling returning for lunch after a good ski class (thank you Kathy Bennett, you most sympathetic, encouraging and easy to understand of instructors). I also loved the peace of the mountain just after sunset, the feeling of being safe and well nurtured at the St. B. The hotel has the magic ability to make its guests feel good and Cuisine St. Bernard has been a joyful exciting project to work on from start to finish.

# INDEX

▲

# THANKS AND ACKNOWLEDGMENTS

Jean, there wouldn't have been a book without you. You are a source of inspiration—not just because your answering machine message ends with 'so much to do, so little time', said with a smile in your voice.

So many people to thank, so little space...

Claude, thank you—not just for being a most patient Publisher Extraordinaire—but also for writing the very fine Kachina Peak story. Peter, your photos capture it all.

I am grateful to the fabulous St. B. chefs for trusting me with their stories and recipes, putting up with questions and nagging emails. In alphabetical order: Claude Gohard, Randy Stabler, Cindie White, Chris White, Steve White, Patrick Yu, Yann Yven. I have tried to do your recipes justice.

I also want to thank Evan Blish, Michael Kierst, Greg Jaramillo, Becky Montoya, Giovanna Hammer, Kathy Humphries, and Pierre-André Thébault.

Thank you to Rick Romancito, The Taos News, for the Ledoux Street photograph on pp 142-3.

A very special thank you to Elise Waters Olonia for her suggestions, help, and picture research.

Un merci du fond du cœur à mon amie de toujours Amina Roessiger.

Special thanks: to Melissa Ames and to Hilary Ames at Box Canyon, a home from home office, for welcoming me, and keeping me informed and entertained; to Kathleen Knox, Executive Director, Taos School of Music; Gordon Briner, Taos Ski Valley General Manager; to 2010 School of Music young artist, violinist Robyn Bollinger, my breakfast companion.

I am grateful to St. B. guests, for their insights and stories (first names only, in alphabetical order): Arron, Barbara, Bruce, Cyndy, Jerry, Jillana, John, Kevin, Lee, Lillian, Murray, Valerie.

I thank Karen and Oliver Perin for introducing me to Aspen and its Music Festival for research purposes, then driving me to the St. B. via Independence Pass. You Americans call everything 'just down the road...'.

Nearer home in London, thank you for encouragement to Frances Fedden, Shirlee Kay, Michele Kurland, Elizabeth Mckay and Lalage Percival. I mustn't forget Bosie and Stella MacIvor. In Saint Malo, thank you to Raphaël Naudin for checking on progress.

Thank you to the talented duo, Bernardo Dominguez and 'grace under pressure' Paola Ferrarotti at Walford Wilkie.

And a very big thank you to my old friend Lewis for his professional all-round support in the final stages of the project.

*Marie-Pierre Moine*

*Hotel St. Bernard*
*PO Box 88*
*(shipping address: 112 Sutton Place)*
*Taos Ski Valley*
*New Mexico 87525*
*Phone - 575.776.2251*

*www.stbernardtaos.com*
*stbhotel@newmex.com*

*Taos Ski Valley*
*www.skitaos.org*

Published by Arundel Press
50 Fifth Avenue
London W10 4DN
United Kingdom

Publisher Claude Roessiger

Copyright text ©Marie-Pierre Moine
Photography ©Peter Lamont

Editor Lewis Esson
Indexer Pat Jacobs

Design & Art Direction: Walford Wilkie Limited
Printed and bound by New Island Printing Co., Ltd, Hong Kong

▲